THE
HOARDER
IN
YOU

THE
HOARDER
IN
YOU

HOW TO LIVE A HAPPIER, HEALTHIER, UNCLUTTERED LIFE

Dr. Robin Zasio

RODALE.

Rodale books may be purchased for business or promotional use or for special sales. For information, please write to:
Special Markets Department, Rodale, Inc., 733 Third Avenue, New York, NY 10017

Printed in the United States of America
Rodale Inc. makes every effort to use acid-free ♾, recycled paper ♻.

Book design by Christopher Rhoads

Library of Congress Cataloging-in-Publication Data

Zasio, Robin.
    The hoarder in you : how to live a happier, healthier, uncluttered life / Robin Zasio.
        p.   cm.
    ISBN 978–1–60961–131–6   hardcover
    1. Compulsive hoarding—Popular works.   2. Obsessive-compulsive disorder—
Popular works.   3. Self-care, Health—Popular works.   I. Title.
RC569.5.H63Z37   2011
616.85'227—dc23   2011030331

Distributed to the trade by Macmillan

2   4   6   8   10   9   7   5   3   hardcover

We inspire and enable people to improve their lives and the world around them.
www.rodalebooks.com

This book is dedicated to all of those individuals who struggle with clutter and compulsive hoarding; whose desire is to cultivate a more healthy relationship to their possessions. Know that you are not alone.

Contents

INTRODUCTION

Not long ago, I was sitting at my vanity getting ready for my day. It was very early on a Monday morning, which is always my busiest day of the week. On this particular day, I was not going into the office, but heading directly to my client Kate's house. This was to be the first time that Kate allowed me inside. We'd worked together off and on for months in my clinic, The Anxiety Treatment Center of Sacramento, but until now she'd been very resistant to letting me see exactly the state of her environment. She was on my mind as I applied makeup and fixed my hair.

Kate herself hadn't contacted me initially; rather, it had been her husband, who told me he could no longer live in their home, which he indicated had once been a beautiful showplace. They seemed well matched: Married for the first time in their forties, neither had children and both had always wanted to travel the world. After only 2 months of marriage, Kate's father passed away and left her a significant trust, which was sizable enough to support both of them for the rest of their lives. It was a wonderful opportunity for the two to realize their dreams of adventure.

The death of Kate's father triggered something in her. Instead of preparing for their trip and investing her inheritance carefully, Kate began shopping with abandon, spending large amounts of money on clothing and other items. Her shopping habit quickly developed into compulsive hoarding. Within a year, her husband, who had desperately tried to understand what Kate was going through, was beside himself with frustration.

As I was getting ready to see Kate that morning, I opened the top right drawer of my vanity (which, like my home in general, is well organized) to reach for a cotton swab and realized there weren't any left. I began pulling open the other drawers in search of the new box I'd recently bought. One drawer held my blow-dryer; another had some first aid cream and bandages. And then, like I've done hundreds of times in the past 8 years I've lived in my home, I opened That Makeup Drawer.

THAT MAKEUP DRAWER

This particular drawer is filled with a jumble of cosmetics, some of which I've had for 2 decades—literally since I was in my early twenties, when I graduated from college. There are crumbling eye shadows in colors I haven't worn in years, and dried-up eye liners, pencils, and lipsticks that I loved when I purchased them (though after applying them for the first time, realized they weren't right for me). Rather than throwing away the useless lipsticks, which felt like a waste, I thought, "What if I need them? You never know . . . " and dumped them in the drawer with the rest of the cast-off cosmetics. I knew I'd likely never use any of these items—and for health reasons, should not use any of them—and yet, as of this writing, That Makeup Drawer remains full. Any time I think of going through it to get rid of stuff, the urge to close the drawer and avoid it is much stronger than my will to clean it out.

The irony was not lost on me that here I was, a clinical psychologist and an expert on the treatment of compulsive hoarding, irrationally unable to get rid of items that would do no one any good. I asked myself why I couldn't toss outdated blush that was too dry to apply, but I already knew the answer: for the exact same reasons my clients say they can't get rid of the stuff that clutters their homes to the point that their houses are practically uninhabitable. I had no time to dwell on that, though. I had work to do. I quickly closed the drawer and left for Kate's house.

As I drove up her driveway, I saw a perfectly manicured yard and walkway that led to a two-story brick home. I rang the bell and immediately heard a crashing sound. "Is everything okay in there?" I shouted. I heard Kate's voice call out, "Yes, I just ran into something."

Minutes later Kate came to the door, apologized for keeping me waiting, and expressed humiliation and embarrassment over the condition of her home. "I really don't feel good about you seeing the place like this," she said, clearly anxious. I reassured her that I would in no way judge her and that I was there to help. I reminded her that we were a team, and that this was the next step in her therapy process.

Up until now, Kate had been bringing items to sort through at the clinic, so that I could teach her the tools she needed to begin letting go of things on her own at home. It can take a few months before a client who compulsively hoards is ready for a therapist to visit her home, to get a firsthand visual of the severity of the problem, and exactly how this condition is affecting her environment. Even though we had developed a rapport and a supportive therapeutic relationship, it is quite common for a client to feel extreme anxiety the first time I visit his or her home. Reminding clients of my nonjudgmental approach often helps them become comfortable enough to invite me in.

Stepping into the entryway, it was clear that Kate had been shopping aggressively for many months. While there was not an ounce of trash in sight (some hoarded homes contain a mixture of trash and usable objects), the house was filled with shopping bags that had not been unpacked, mail-order boxes, and clothing with the tags still attached. While she had promised her husband repeatedly that she would get things "put away," he noticed that Kate just kept bringing in more stuff. This is consistent with many people that I work with: They have good intentions, but lack the ability to follow through with them. Kate had multiple organizing systems, such as bins and plastic drawer sets, stacked on top of one another, ready to be filled, but because of the volume of stuff in the house, there was no place to put them, let alone put things *in* them.

Kate suffered from compulsive hoarding, a debilitating anxiety condition in which a person is trapped in a prison of his or her possessions. People who are compulsive hoarders come from all ages, races, ethnicities, and religious backgrounds and live all over the world. What all of these individuals have in common is a compulsive drive to acquire, and a crippling inability to get rid of things they no longer need, to the point where their living spaces can't be used in a healthy, functional manner.

I've visited the homes of people whose spouses had left them because they could no longer bear to live amid so much stuff (including garbage); those who were in danger of losing their children to protective service agencies because the unsanitary state of their homes put their children at risk; and people whose entire homes were filled, floor to ceiling, with stacks of molding newspapers and magazines. I've worked with people who ate breakfast, lunch, and dinner with their families on their beds or other makeshift tables formed by an overturned box or two, because their dining area and coffee table were piled high with things so that there was no other place to eat. One man I met had so many ceramic dogs all over his home—he preferred them to people—that there was no place to sit. I have a very limited sense of smell, the result of a horseback riding accident when I was a child, yet I have felt my eyes tear up at the powerful odor of urine or feces or rotting food.

That morning, Kate and I decided to work on her bedroom. As we sorted through a pile of clothing—much of which was brand-new but two sizes too small for Kate—I asked her why she kept piles of clothes that didn't fit.

"Well, it's too late to return them, and it feels like a waste—I spent money on them," she replied. I asked her when the last time was that these clothes might have fit her, and she replied that it had been years since she'd been that size. "But they might fit me again, and so I save them just in case," she said. I asked her how she felt when she saw those too-small clothes. Did they make her feel good about herself? She admitted they did not, that they were a reminder that she'd put on weight. That led to a discussion of how the "just in case" thinking was part of what led to her house being hoarded, and that the real likelihood that she'd wear those exact clothes again, even if she did lose weight, was small, as they'd be out of style by that time. I suggested that the clothes and the clutter added to her stress level, because they caused conflict with her husband and made her feel as though she failed by gaining weight. While Kate felt initial anxiety at the thought of getting rid of that pile, she was eventually able to let go of the clothes and donate most of them to Goodwill.

Driving home from Kate's house, I thought about That Makeup Drawer. The fact was, every time I opened it, I felt a little wave of angst and disappointment with myself for not doing anything about it. Besides, all that makeup that I'd bought and never used—what a waste of money! And that space could be better used for something else. Why had I let it go for so long?

I sounded just like Kate. Those thoughts—that it would be wasteful to throw away something I spent money on, or that I might need it one day, or that it's still perfectly good and useful—are the exact same thoughts that run through the minds of people who suffer from compulsive hoarding. Of course, my makeup drawer doesn't get in the way of my living a happy and productive life. But it occurred to me at that moment that many of us have a relationship with our things that could be improved upon. We are all on a continuum, from the man who saves nothing because he can't stand even a bit of disorganization, to the guy whose house is tidy enough but whose garage is a museum of unfinished projects and boxes of historical artifacts, to a woman like Kate, or someone with a more severe case. If we all have similar irrational thoughts about our things (I've been known to buy more than one of something I didn't need because it was "a good deal," another common rationalization for excessive acquiring), perhaps there is something we can all learn from the treatment of people at the extreme end of this continuum.

That's how this book came to be. To the extent that clutter gets in the way of living in the kind of environment we'd like to be living in and leaves us feeling stressed or remiss, we can all improve our relationships to our possessions. Our clutter not only takes up physical space in our homes and offices, but it also occupies needless mental space—space that could be used to enjoy the lives we've worked so hard to build. I believe that's one of the reasons the A&E show *Hoarders,* on which I am a contributing psychologist, is so popular. Of course there is the shock factor of looking into the lives of people with an extreme and highly visible problem. But I also hear from viewers who say that they see a little bit of themselves or someone they know in these extreme cases, that they can in some way relate to what those who compulsively hoard are going through.

I see it as my mission, both at my clinic and as a public face in the treatment for people struggling with compulsive hoarding, to help foster an environment of compassion around this condition and those who suffer from it. People who hoard don't want to live the way they do; many are working hard to overcome the condition, which is not a character flaw but an anxiety-related issue, the result of differences in brain chemistry that lead to the inability to make decisions about their possessions.

I have a passion to help people improve their lives, and nothing gives me greater pleasure than to help someone work to understand what causes him to acquire and have difficulty letting go, and help him to reorganize his life, both emotionally and in terms of his physical environment. It is rewarding for me to see clients create better relationships with the people they love and begin to live happier lives as a result of treatment. Unfortunately, not everyone can afford to get help, and insurance companies are often reluctant to pay for the services of clinicians, organizers, and other specialists. This book will help those who are struggling with this condition and who don't have access to the kind of help they need.

But you don't need to have a severe problem with clutter or hoarding to benefit from the techniques and tools that I will share in the chapters to come. We all have our version of That Makeup Drawer, whether it's a chaotic office with boxes and boxes of paper, a closet that is packed to the rafters with things we've been dreading going through, an overflowing pantry, or a house that just never seems calm because of the piles on every surface. Clutter affects us not only in a practical way—how much easier might it be to get out the door in the morning if you didn't need to frantically hunt for your sunglasses, and how many fewer arguments would you get into with your spouse if you'd paid that bill on time, the one you put down and forgot about?—but also in an emotional sense. An uncluttered space helps to allow for a less cluttered mind. Getting to the bottom of why we live the way we do is the first step.

I'm glad you'll be taking this journey with me.

THE
HOARDER
IN
YOU

CHAPTER 1

PACK RATS, CLUTTERERS, AND COMPULSIVE HOARDERS

YOU WOULD NEVER HAVE SUSPECTED that Joan suffered from compulsive hoarding. When I first met her at my office in Sacramento, I saw an impeccably dressed African American woman of 50, who I knew from the referral was a highly regarded administrator at an insurance company, the model of efficiency and attention to detail at work for 2 decades.

The first time I saw her home, however, was a very different story. Joan was at Level 4 (out of 5) on the Clutter Hoarding Scale, an assessment tool devised by the National Study Group of Chronic Disorganization (NSGCD) in St. Louis. In broad terms, someone at Level 4 would have significant difficulty cleaning a home without professional help; conditions of the home are unsanitary or otherwise hazardous (food is often rotting on counters, and rodents and insects may be visible in multiple locations); rooms in the home are so packed with objects that they are unusable for their original purpose; there's mold and structural damage to the home; and when pets are present, there is accumulated animal waste. Joan's house met all of these conditions. It was hard to imagine that this calm, confident woman could emerge every day from such a place.

The first thing I noticed about Joan's house was the smell. Even with my impaired sense of smell, the odor of ammonia and feces was overwhelming. The cats' litter box, which was in the dining room, was overflowing, but a walk through the house made it clear that the two cats had long since given up on it and were urinating and defecating everywhere. Joan's three bedrooms were unusable—piles of clothes and books, many contaminated with cat waste, were everywhere, and disorganized to-do piles of bills, receipts, and laundry covered the living room.

In the kitchen, the counters were piled with old food and dirty, empty food containers. Canned goods and packaged foods overflowed from the pantry because Joan had bought multiples of the same items. The freezer was so full that it had frozen shut. Gnats flew everywhere. When I pulled open the freezer door and peered inside, I saw countless dead insects that had somehow worked their way into the seal. I pointed this out to Joan, who didn't seem terribly bothered by it; she said something vague about meaning to call the exterminator.

I'd seen worse homes in my years of treating people who hoard, but what I remember most about Joan's house is the plastic bags filled with cat feces that were sitting by the litter box, leaning up against the sliding glass door to the backyard. Apparently, Joan would scoop the contents of the litter box into the bag, intend to place the bags into the garbage, and either forget or find herself unable to lift it. She said she was always meaning to call someone to help her throw it out, but she never did. As a result, bags of cat waste sat in the living room. Joan, like many who compulsively hoard, had a system, albeit one that didn't work well. She was full of good intentions, but the time to take care of all the things she meant to simply never came. There were always, as with many of us, more important things to do.

Joan's case exemplifies to me many of the things people don't understand about hoarding. Many people judge hoarders harshly, believing them to be lazy, unsanitary, uncaring, selfish, self-absorbed, or narcissistic.* Joan's personality couldn't be further from any of these traits. She was desperate to live differently—she just didn't know how—and she needed help. Joan completed the 6-week Intensive Outpatient Program at my clinic, which involves extensive hours of therapy and home visits. While her home wasn't perfectly free of clutter when she was discharged from the program, she now lives a very different life than she did before treatment. She currently works with a therapist one-on-one, and she continues to improve.

In my practice and on the A&E show *Hoarders,* I work with people like Joan, who suffer from compulsive hoarding, an anxiety condition in which individuals are simply unable to prevent themselves from accumulating and saving oftentimes shocking amounts of stuff, most of which an outside observer would consider useless garbage. Some 3 million people in this country are thought to compulsively hoard, but I believe that number is a gross underestimate due to the shame, guilt, embarrassment, and fear that prevent many people from seeking help.

In extreme hoarding situations, people may live in squalor, with conditions so unsanitary and hazardous that their physical safety and that of their loved ones and pets is at risk. I have seen contamination from food, garbage, and human and animal waste eat through the walls and floorboards of a home, leaving gaping holes and wood riddled with insects. It's difficult to imagine how someone could think a platter of food with visible mold could ever be worth saving.

You have likely heard of the legendary Collyer brothers, two wealthy eccentrics who were found dead in their brownstone by New York City police and firemen in 1947 amidst their 130 tons of belongings. (E. L. Doctorow novelized their lives in a book released in 2009,

---

* I would like to be clear that I am using the term *hoarder,* and later *clutterer,* not to label someone who is suffering from compulsive hoarding or who has a tendency toward clutter, but rather as a shorthand way of referring to that person. I dislike the use of labels because labels are limiting and seem to obscure the potential for change that each one of us has inside of us. In using these terms, I am in no way indicating that a compulsive hoarder, clutterer, or even pack rat is the entirety of who that person is. It simply describes behaviors that impact the person's life.

and for years, mothers in New York City cited their example—"You don't want to wind up like the Collyer brothers, do you?"—to motivate their children to clean their rooms.) Extreme and sometimes tragic cases of compulsive hoarding continue to be reported regularly. Just last year, a Las Vegas woman who was reported missing by her husband was found dead 4 months later in her own home, buried under a pile of her belongings. Law enforcement and investigators had searched the place several times. "For our dogs to go through that house and not find something should be indicative of the tremendous environmental challenges they faced," a police spokesperson said. It is impossible to walk into a home like that and not wonder, "How did things get this bad, and how can a person live this way?"

The answer is complicated, as complicated as the minds of people who suffer from compulsive hoarding, a condition that can lead to severe isolation, depression, and physical degeneration, as well as interfere with someone's ability to earn a living and function in society. One reason people can live like that for so long is because they become habituated to their environment. That is, they simply get used to it—they adjust, accommodate to it, and work around the obstacles. Randy O. Frost, PhD, who studies compulsive hoarding at Smith College, calls this symptom clutter blindness. It's an apt term, because those who hoard often do not see what the rest of us do when we look at the same pile of stuff. They see lots of useful possessions or rooms that are "a bit disorganized," while we see complete chaos and mountains of randomly collected items. It is a problem of perception.

Sometimes it is not until an outsider comes in—be it a friend, someone like me who is there to help, or an agent from the state or county who is evaluating whether children or animals can live safely in a home—that the wall of denial that many hoarders have built around themselves can be broken down. Sometimes, but not always, they see the way they've been living through others' eyes and realize that their lives have spun out of control. On other occasions, sadly, they are unable to recognize the severity of their problem.

A CLUTTERED LIFE

I'm like many people in that I'm far more likely to want to give the bathroom an extra scrubbing, or perhaps finally go through that stack of junk mail on the side table, if I have company coming over. I am a very organized person, and somewhat private; I don't want the world to see my mess, the minutia of my life. I like to present a polished exterior, and my home is a reflection of that, by and large. Of course, a few piles that need to be sorted through, or even a crazy messy laundry room where random holiday decorations and outgrown bicycles are stored isn't a big deal, and many people have messy basements, garages, or attics where they keep things. Still, we can all do with less mess, and I think what we have in common with those who are compulsive hoarders is a large part of the appeal of the A&E show *Hoarders*, and why there has been so much coverage of the condition in recent years. Fortunately, this media exposure has led many more people to seek treatment because they know that they are not alone.

I think the majority of us see a tiny bit of ourselves reflected in hoarders. And as you'll soon discover in the chapters to come, the way hoarders think about their possessions is in many ways not terribly different from the way non-hoarders approach the stuff in their lives. (For the purposes of this book, I will refer to people who are not suffering from compulsive hoarding, but who have a problem with clutter, as "non-hoarders" or sometimes "clutterers.") I can't tell you how many times I've asked my clients why they can't get rid of an individual item, and their answer is, "Because I'm afraid if I throw it out, I'll need it in the future." On other occasions I hear, "Because it would be wasteful to get rid of something that could still be used," or "It was such a good deal, I couldn't pass it up," or "This item was given to me by someone I love, and I don't feel right about throwing it out." Those are very common reasons to acquire or keep things— who doesn't think some version of those thoughts when going through his or her belongings?

What differentiates someone with this condition from a non-hoarder, of course, is that a hoarder is unable to take into account important factors like whether keeping an item may cause him more harm than good. The inability to make rational decisions about whether to keep things or let go of them; the degree of anxiety experienced when trying to sort through personal effects; and the sheer volume of belongings are all hallmarks of a compulsive hoarder. But the thought processes of a person on the far end of the hoarding spectrum and the thought processes of a person like me are not so different. While there are clinical differences between people who suffer from compulsive hoarding and those who are not struggling with this condition, when it comes to some of the behaviors and thought patterns, it is to some extent a matter of degree.

For that reason, I believe we can all benefit from gaining a better understanding of this condition and how it's treated, even if your home has only an average amount of clutter and mess. It's easy to see how clutter—even if it's not on the level of the Collyer brothers—can interfere with your life in very practical ways, and cause you to waste many hours of your week searching for things that you need. It can also make it difficult to be calm and present and enjoy your life to the fullest, and cause unnecessary stress and frustration.

Teresa's story perfectly illustrates how too much stuff can add stress to your life, even if you don't have an actual hoarding problem, but struggle with clutter, like so many more of us. A nurse and the mother of two boys, Teresa, age 43, is always panicked in the morning, no matter how early she sets her alarm. She allots sufficient time to shower and get her kids ready for school, but inevitably she can't find one essential item she needs before heading out the door. One day it's her sunglasses; another, it's her passport, which is required to complete a tax form at work. It's not uncommon for her husband to find Teresa, 5 minutes after she should have left to drop off the kids, dressed in her uniform, on her hands and knees, cursing like a sailor and searching through dust bunnies under her bed for the left shoe that matches the one on her right foot.

Teresa's house isn't terribly messy—just the usual explosion of stuff that comes with living with two sons and never having time to put things away properly—but it drives her batty. Teresa is a perfectionist: She can't think of the perfect place to put things, the perfect system to keep everything organized, so she procrastinates on organizing and frequently cannot find what she needs. More often than not, Teresa gives up, slips on a second-choice pair of shoes that she's not happy with, and races out the door. Once at school, her boys race from the car to their classrooms to beat the morning bell. Teresa sits in the parking lot, feeling frazzled and stressed, and applies her makeup in the rearview mirror.

If you asked Teresa if she likes her morning routine, she'd say no, but that she's too busy to constantly clean up, and the amount of stuff that a family of four requires is simply too much for her to keep under control. She does what she can to contain the chaos, but has largely surrendered to it. Frankly, she'd rather spend time with her kids and relax on the weekend than organize.

Still, living the way she does affects Teresa and her family on a daily basis—she's overwhelmed, often late, and never feels quite together. There's always something she should be doing to get her house in order, and it weighs on her, so she can't just relax at home after work. Every pile is a reminder of a job not yet done. If her house were in better shape and if she could find a way to function more efficiently within it, she would without a doubt be happier, and so would her family.

LEARNING FROM THE EXTREME CASES

Because we are all on a continuum of clutter, it can be helpful to know more about what compulsive hoarding is and how the condition manifests. Surprisingly, it was not until 1996 that psychologists Randy O. Frost and Tamara Hartl proposed a theoretical framework to describe hoarding. In their model, they suggested that people who hoard experience a combination of information-processing deficits, distorted beliefs about and emotional attachments to their possessions, and difficulty with organization.

To break it down further, information-processing deficits can make it difficult to make good decisions about what to bring into the home and what to let go of. As a result, for compulsive hoarders, there is an excessive accumulation of objects that begins to take over, room by room. Dysfunctional beliefs about the worth of their stuff further prevent them from discarding or letting go ("I can fix it"; "Someone may want it"; "If I let this go, I will regret it."), ultimately resulting in their keeping and holding on to more stuff than the house can sustain. Problems with organization, categorization, and attention contribute to the hoarding behavior, and it's not long before the house is no longer functional, personal safety is compromised, and relationships are impacted.

Further, while there is nothing wrong with having lots of possessions, those who struggle with hoarding are not able to balance what comes into the home with what goes out. A related phenomenon, identified by Fred Penzel, PhD, is called *pseudo-hoarding*. This is when people have difficulty throwing things out not because they are invested in saving the objects, but because they fear there will be something valuable mixed in with the trash that will be accidentally discarded. Their homes look hoarded, but these people would not be classified as compulsive hoarders.

Attaching deep emotional significance to possessions is not, in and of itself, abnormal. But whereas you or I might not want to part with a childhood teddy bear that once brought us comfort, someone who is dealing with compulsive hoarding might attach even greater emotional importance to such items, and to a much greater range and number of things, sometimes attributing to them human emotions, such as imagining how the bear would feel if it was thrown out. A hoarder will often imagine how she herself would feel if she were discarded, and find the thought of inflicting those painful feelings on even an inanimate object unbearable. Someone who hoards may also attribute emotional significance to items much more readily, so there are many, many items she becomes deeply attached to. In some cases, a hoarder may feel as though the object is a part of their identity, and to discard it would be like throwing out a part of themselves. Whereas non-hoarders might have a few items that they cherish and take special care of, a person who hoards might feel just as attached to the piles and boxes and bags of stuff that seem dispensable to others as she is to a special memento.

I treated a woman named Jennifer who was a beautiful, capable mother of grown children. She had lost her mother a year before we met, and Jennifer found herself unable to part with rooms full of items that had belonged to her mother (who had also hoarded). The loss of her mother was "devastating," she said, and although she held a job and was entirely functional in every other way, the thought of sorting through or parting with any of her mother's things was more than she could handle. Meanwhile, she herself had accumulated excessive stuff or things over the years, so there were piles of clothing and garbage all over her home. Jennifer had also been keeping dogs (14 of them), whose waste could be found in every room.

The result was that she hadn't seen her floor in 2 years, and she was completely isolated from the outside world. When her children came over to visit, they had no place to sit and frequently found themselves stepping in dog feces. They were so angry and frustrated that after a while they stopped coming inside the house and would only ring the doorbell and say hello from outside. One of them stopped speaking to Jennifer altogether. I was called when there was so much damage to the house from the hoard (broken windows and panes) that it needed to be cleared so a repairman could fix it. He also needed to fix the leaky roof, which the hoard prevented him from doing.

She and I, along with a cleaning crew, sorted through her things, room by room, item by item. There were many relics that she agonized over putting in the trash. She was self-deprecating about her problem, and she laughed and put on a brave face when she felt embarrassed or sad. In order to help her, I had to encourage her to not laugh away the feelings of grief over her mother's death, to let those feelings surface, and to acknowledge that the way she'd been living had been getting in the way of her relationships with her children. Her need to avoid the emotions that she knew would arise in making decisions about her mother's things was so strong that she was paralyzed at the thought of cleaning up.

After days of digging out, we uncovered Jennifer's Barbie collection. These dolls had provided her with some of the happiest play memories she had as a child, but they were destroyed by water damage, dust, and dirt. The irony—that she had saved these dolls because they were important to her, but that in saving more things than she could care for, she destroyed the dolls—was not lost on her. She felt like she'd let her Barbies down by not protecting them and keeping them safely in their containers. Her daughter was through helping, and at that point, Jennifer seemed more concerned about the dolls' feelings than those of her children. I see this quite often: The attachment to things seems more important to a hoarder than her attachment to the people in her life. As a result, her fear of losing something valuable results in the loss of many valuable things and relationships.

The disorganized thinking that is a characteristic of compulsive hoarding is partly what leads to the inability to make good decisions about what to keep and what to toss, or whether or not to acquire something in the first place. Oftentimes a hoarder has difficulty paying attention or staying on task, and may even be suffering from attention deficit hyperactivity disorder.

Other people who hoard might have problems with categorization, meaning they have a difficult time sorting their possessions into types of objects, and so deciding what to do with each item becomes incredibly time consuming and feels overwhelming. Joan, for example, had her "to-do" piles, but rather than a stack of mail that needed to be opened, bills that needed to be paid, a pair of shoes that needed to be returned to the store, and a basket of laundry that needed to be washed, her "to-do" pile contained all of these things, because in her mind, they all went together—they were all things she needed to take care of more or less immediately. When she came home, she'd put her keys on top of her "to-do" pile, which makes a certain kind of sense if you follow her logic (her keys would be where she was most likely to look, among the things she needed to take care of) but practically guaranteed they'd be buried in no time.

Still other hoarders have trouble with procrastination. That's another irony: Many people who hoard are perfectionists who are paralyzed into inaction because they cannot decide on the ideal place to put something, and as a result, their homes are the farthest thing from perfect. The anxiety they experience when they consider that they might put an item in the "wrong" place, or in trying to decide what the "right" place is, makes them avoid dealing with the item altogether. Hoarders will put an item somewhere, anywhere, as a temporary measure, until they can figure out the right place—but they never find that place, and so the hoard grows and causes enormous stress not just to the person who is hoarding, but to anyone who lives in the household.

One of my clients, Sierra, had so much stuff and was so disorganized that she'd walk from the car with a bag of groceries—often perishables, like meats and dairy—and put them down wherever she had room in her house. Occasionally she'd even set them outside the back door "temporarily." The problem was that her home was filled to the ceiling with stuff (it was so unlivable that her husband had divorced her a year earlier). Sierra would think, "I'll come get that stuff and put it away as soon as I find the right place." But that usually didn't happen. How long the food sat out varied, but much of the time it spoiled. Sierra and I had many discussions about whether specific items were reasonable to keep. While some of the food might have been edible, I'd argue that it wasn't worth the risk. Sierra felt throwing it away was wasteful.

Not surprisingly, people who hoard also often have symptoms of depression. This is understandable, when you think of what their environment and sense of powerlessness does to them: Having a home that isn't presentable can lead to shame, social isolation, and loneliness. Even if a person is clutter blind, he often knows on some level that the way he lives is not how non-hoarders live, and so he avoids having people over. What's more, when the halls and stairwells of a home are so cluttered that there's no room to walk around, the opportunity for physical exertion is very limited, leading to sluggishness and in many cases the worsening of health problems, which in itself can lead to or compound depression.

Barry—who, along with his wife, Melissa, suffered from compulsive hoarding—is an example of how the condition can worsen depression and other health issues. Barry was in his midforties and had been in a car accident that left him with chronic back pain. His apartment was so packed with things that he spent most of his time on the couch watching TV. Their apartment was cluttered mainly with boxes of possessions he'd had all his life and that he carried with him each time he moved. The boxes contained a variety of items—train sets, clothing that no longer fit, several jackets from when he lived on the East Coast (items that he no longer needed living in California), and tools from a job that he had 5 years earlier. He could part with none of these items and continued to buy more of the same. He had the idea that he and Melissa "might" move back east, so he would go online and purchase more cold weather clothing, just in case. He also bought tools on eBay, in the hope that one day he'd be able to work on cars again, even though his back problems made that unlikely. These new items would remain in their boxes, which would pile up all the way to the ceiling.

Barry was on disability and felt so depressed about his physical health that he lacked the will and the energy to get up to unpack the boxes and organize his things. Because he rarely moved around or engaged with others, his muscles, body, and mind continued to atrophy. He prepared all his food in the microwave (as evidenced by the empty packages stacked next to the couch that also served as his bed). Barry said he couldn't throw away the food packaging because he might want to go back and read the ingredients on the packages. When I asked him if he ever actually read the ingredients, he said no.

Melissa, meanwhile, shopped to occupy her time, mostly for clothing. Interestingly enough, Melissa had no history of hoarding until she met Barry; I believe her hoarding was a response to the depressive environment in their apartment. She needed a distraction from her marriage, a way to make up for the joy that she wasn't getting from her relationship with Barry. The thrill of acquiring new things made her feel good, and it was something she had in common with her husband. But Barry and Melissa were at risk of losing their apartment because it was unsafe. Each blamed the other for having too much stuff. Ultimately, part of the therapeutic process included both of them taking responsibility for their acquiring behaviors and individually developing healthy spending habits that were controlled and managed.

There are also a small number of people who hoard animals rather than things per se. It's not known exactly how many people hoard animals, but it's most likely a small percentage of those who hoard. In animal hoarding, the person becomes very attached to her pets for company and for an emotional outlet, but she tends to have so many that she can't properly take care of them all, and her environment suffers for it. She also tends to deny the suffering and harmful conditions in which the animals are living and the medical problems that they may visibly have. Someone is considered to have a problem with compulsive animal hoarding if there are too many animals for the person to take proper care of; if the animals don't have adequate food, water, or shelter; or if they don't have adequate medical care or attention.

WHO FALLS INTO COMPULSIVE HOARDING?

It can be very frustrating for sufferers of this condition to not be able to understand why they are compelled to hoard, and I am often asked, is it nature or nurture? In other words, is someone genetically predisposed to hoarding, or does it have to do with the way the person was raised or events that have transpired in her life? But looking at it as simply nature versus nurture is a bit too simplistic. The condition has both genetic and environmental influences, but even taking those into account, it's not really possible to accurately predict whether a person will end up hoarding.

We do know that genetic factors contribute to those who are compulsive hoarders, and in situations in which there is a strong family history, it is likely that this predisposition is contributing to the hoarding behavior. It could also be a sign that hoarding is a learned response to managing anxiety—if a child sees her mother holding on to things as a way of dealing with loss, she may learn that doing so is a way to manage her own feelings. Most experts agree that it is likely that each of these influences plays a role. If someone is genetically predisposed to hoarding, it is going to be harder for her to resist developing the tendency herself if she is exposed to environmental factors. Sometimes we also see a history of other anxiety-related conditions in the families of people who hoard.

That said, there are plenty of people who grow up in homes with parents who hoard who do not become compulsive hoarders themselves. These people may even react in opposition to the environmental influences of their childhood and may have a low tolerance for clutter. Or perhaps they simply aren't genetically predisposed to hoard. Ultimately, compulsive hoarding is a complex condition, requiring specialized treatment that needs to be tailored to meet and address each individual's circumstances.

Generally speaking, behaviors consistent with hoarding develop early in life, yet people don't tend to seek treatment until their fifties. This condition is believed to affect men more frequently than women, although in my clinic, I find that more women than men seek help. Compulsive hoarding appears to become more pronounced later in life, probably for circumstantial reasons. For instance, when someone goes to college, his hoarding tendencies tend to be contained because he's living in one room or with a roommate whose irritation with the clutter helps him keep it in check. Later, perhaps he meets someone and gets married, and the presence of a partner initially has a positive influence. Eventually, though, a person's loved ones come to accept a certain amount of clutter—Dad is really into tools and has taken over the garage—and, like the hoarder himself, become habituated to the environment.

The living conditions typically spiral downward gradually. When children are grown and out of the house, a person who hoards can become more isolated. An empty nest means he has more room to hoard, and often he stops having people over. The lack of outside perspective from visitors means that he can remain in denial about his home, and the stuff keeps accumulating. As in the case of Jennifer, whose daughter came to help her clear the house, a hoarder's grown children are often stunned by the way their parent lives. Spouses frequently get fed up with living in clutter and threaten to leave if the house isn't cleaned.

I'm also often asked if hoarding is the result of deprivation in childhood. For example, if a person grows up very poor and without the things she needs, does that make her more likely to hoard her possessions as an adult? That can happen—I've seen people who have worried that there was never enough food to eat and now overstock and hoard food—but in my experience, deprivation is not generally the trigger. There are people who hoard who grew up with everything they needed and more, and there are many people who grew up with very little and don't struggle with compulsive hoarding.

Hoarding is also not necessarily a result of a trauma, although if someone has a tendency toward compulsive hoarding, a trauma can trigger the condition, and there is research that shows that the more traumatic life events the subjects had, the more severe their hoarding problems were. It is well known, for instance, that Holocaust survivors were seen to hoard food, money, clothing, and other items. Jennie, a 50-year-old mother I worked with who had lost her infant son inexplicably through crib death, stands out in my mind. I don't believe she would have started to compulsively hoard had she not had a severe trauma that caused her life to take a turn for the worse. Another heartbreaking case was Bill, a respected police officer, who was called to the scene of a fatal car accident one night to find that it was his own daughter who had been hit by a drunk driver. He was shattered. After taking a leave of absence, he could not resume work because anytime he was called to a traffic accident, he feared that another one of his family members might be involved. Bill simply couldn't pull himself out of his sadness and became a recluse. His food was delivered, and he shopped online to avoid having to drive anywhere. Bill limited opportunities for family members to visit and began to occupy his time with collecting Incan artifacts. The thrill of finding a special piece or a good deal would overtake him, and he filled his house with these items, many of which were stacked in boxes in rooms that were no longer accessible. It wasn't long before the inside of Bill's house was only accessible via narrow paths running through it. Out of concern, his family finally threatened to report him to Adult Protective Services unless he sought help.

A Condition, Not a Character Flaw

The hardest part about my public role in helping people who suffer from compulsive hoarding is the judgments that are heaped upon them. On online forums on compulsive hoarding and my own Facebook page, I've seen people who lash out, calling those with compulsive hoarding cruel and hurtful names, from crazy to lazy and many in between. Are some hoarders lazy? Of course. But so are many non-hoarders. You can be both lazy and have mental health issues. I have met many people with this condition who want very much to get better and improve their lives but simply don't know how and/or cannot do it alone.

There is also evidence that people with compulsive hoarding have brain chemistry abnormalities that impair their ability to make rational decisions. Sanjaya Saxena, MD, professor in the department of psychiatry at the University of California, San Diego, and a world-renowned neuropsychiatrist specializing in obsessive-complusive disorder (OCD), and his team have used positron emission tomography (PET) imaging to discover distinct patterns of brain activity that are associated with compulsive hoarding. Their studies suggest that compulsive hoarders are more likely to have mild atrophy or an unusual shape to their frontal lobes, which is the part of the brain associated with executive functions and decision-making.

Most psychological disorders run on a continuum, from the very mild to the extreme. You don't have to be paralyzed by major depression, unable to get out of bed or overwhelmed with thoughts of suicide, to relate to feeling down or in a rut, or even have a period of depression yourself. You needn't have generalized anxiety disorder to be familiar with feelings of anxiety or have the occasional sleepless night.

The same is true of compulsive hoarding. We are all on a continuum when it comes to our relationships with our things, from the mild to the extreme, and we all experience varying degrees of distress because of it. This makes intuitive sense, but has also been studied under controlled conditions. Environmental psychology research in the workplace has shown that overall, people prefer an orderly, less cluttered environment, and that a cluttered, disorganized space is associated with higher anxiety and poorer work performance. Interestingly, those who saw a space as more cluttered (even if it was a relatively neat space) felt more anxious in it, which speaks to the fact that one person might be greatly affected by a level of clutter that doesn't bother someone else. One survey (commissioned by Rubbermaid, which makes containers for organizing) found that 91 percent of people are overwhelmed by clutter in their homes at least some of the time, and half don't have friends over because of it; 88 percent wish they had less clutter. In addition, 57 percent report feeling "stressed" and 42 percent are "more anxious" when their house is unorganized or cluttered.

Whether you simply have bags of paperwork and bills that sit in the basement because you don't know what to do with them, or you're like Teresa, and your every morning is a frantic, joyless treasure hunt that starts off your day with too much stress; whether you're someone who lives in a pristine home with a secret closet teeming with things that you're dreading going through; or whether you avoid having people over sometimes because you can't bring yourself to clean, the things I've learned about what we all have in common with compulsive hoarders can help us all live a little freer.

In the chapters that follow, you'll discover where you fall on the continuum and learn how to think about your home and your things differently, so that you can live in an uncluttered space with an uncluttered mind.

CHAPTER 2

OUR LOVE AFFAIR WITH STUFF

OUR THINGS AREN'T MERELY UTILITARIAN objects like the crude weapons and eating implements our ancestors once fashioned out of stone. In our consumerist society, even minimalists have countless catalogs from which to order streamlined accessories to decorate their spare spaces, and of course own far more than they need to survive.

And this can be wonderful. Many of the finer things in life aren't strictly necessary. No one really *needs* a coffee table book of beautiful Ansel Adams nature photography, or a collection of miniature model boats from the turn of the century. Perhaps you need a car, but no one technically needs a beautiful piece of machinery that makes you feel like a rock star when you drive it. Lord knows I don't need my collection of Swarovski crystals—I merely like it. These things give us pleasure when we look at, touch, or use them, and perhaps they remind us of events in our past that fill us with joy or rich memories. Maybe they represent status or achievement; your hard work has given you the means to buy things that bring you pleasure. But could you survive without them? Probably.

However, the proliferation of cool, new, and often mass-produced and affordable stuff makes it easy to have much more than we need, or even more than serves the benign purpose of making us feel good. I think of it as analogous to obesity in this country. There's nothing wrong with enjoying food and having treats, of course. But unlike our ancestors, who had to search for and work to acquire food, which often required extreme physical exertion or travel over great distances, we live in an environment where food is readily available almost all the time, even in the most unusual places. When we stand in the checkout aisle of Staples with our toner cartridge, it's hard to resist grabbing a giant jar of pretzels or bag of chips. The availability of relatively cheap, high-calorie food everywhere we look isn't the only reason people are overweight, but it certainly contributes to the problem.

The same goes for material goods. How many times have you walked into a drugstore for one or two items, and walked out with half a dozen? It happens to me frequently. Perhaps you truly needed more than you thought you did when you entered the store, but odds are you bought an item because it seemed like something you might need, it was a good deal, or it was just plain interesting (gee, I wonder if that pedicure egg-shaped foot callus scraper thing I saw on TV really works?). The next thing you know, you have lots of stuff that you didn't set out to buy, and that stuff comes home with you, cluttering your bathroom. It seems a waste to throw away something that you spent good money on, and so oftentimes, there it sits, even if you don't use it. Almost all of us have far more than we need or could use. That has become the norm in our fortunate, relatively wealthy society.

THE HOARDER'S PERSPECTIVE

Now imagine experiencing the allure of what I just described in the drugstore or in Staples, but magnified by thousands. People who compulsively hoard see value, the potential for use, and meaning in many, many more things than the rest of us do, and because of the anxiety they experience about these objects, they often make impulsive decisions about what they need in the moment. This goes for people who shop in stores as well as those who scavenge at garage sales and rummage through what others have put out on the curb as trash. Most people would look at a stained, frayed old chair with the stuffing coming out, the laminate peeling off, and a leg missing and see an item that isn't worth the effort of refurbishing, even if it's free. A person who hoards, on the other hand, might see its essential form as a chair, and a chair is something someone—anyone—could use. He would minimize the chair's structural and aesthetic problems or even view them as challenges that it would be exciting to overcome. It's a form of excessively distorted optimism, both about the item's potential value as well as the amount of time and energy the person who hoards must devote to making it useful. People who hoard often script the future, but the script is typically not a realistic prediction.

Jason, 32, who came to me for OCD-related issues 2 years ago, is one such person. Jason was on disability from his job as a truck driver and was quite handy at repairing electronics. He would go to garage sales in hopes of getting a good deal on an appliance he could fix or a device that he could take apart and use the parts to rehab another appliance for himself or someone else. Because he wasn't working, he had lots of time to tinker and was consumed in his hunt for good deals. His two-bedroom apartment was already filled with computers, most of which were outdated and would have cost more to repair than to purchase new. His kitchen was piled high with dirty, stained appliances such as blenders, coffeepots, microwaves, and toasters, and even curling irons and blow dryers (he wasn't married and had a shaved head). Jason spent what little money he had on these projects, and was at the limit on his credit cards.

Jason had people in mind who he thought might want these special treasures. If there really had been a market for his items, his thinking would not have been unusual. But Jason's grand ideas of all he could accomplish with his repair projects were not grounded in reality; they were thinking errors, also called cognitive distortions. Questioning some of our strongly held beliefs—the ones that do not serve us and in fact prevent us from moving forward in our lives—is the basic tenet of cognitive behavioral therapy (CBT), the modality that has been shown to be most effective in treating compulsive hoarding. We all have cognitive distortions of one kind or another that contribute to our clutter, and which I will go into in detail in later chapters.

Jason's beliefs were not realistic given his life circumstances, and led him to make poor decisions. On a practical level, he didn't have the money to purchase the parts needed to fix the appliances, and because he had so many, most of them just sat collecting dust. What's more, many of the people that he had in mind to give the appliances to weren't interested in them and didn't need them. He had not been able to give away or sell an item for 6 years. His apartment was filled because the pleasure he felt in the thrill of the kill and his desire to give to others compelled him to keep hunting for treasures that no one else considered valuable.

One of my roles with a patient like this is to talk him through his thinking errors, to help him see that although his beliefs make sense and sound logical to him, they are not, and they contribute to his home being uninhabitable. I also try to suggest other beliefs that he could replace the faulty ones with. Some of Jason's distorted beliefs included "If I see value in it, someone else will," which clearly wasn't the case. He also thought, "If I pass this good deal up and find someone who might be able to use it, I will regret it," which he believed to be true, but because he never actually passed up a good deal, he never got to find out if it was true or not. The thought of passing up the deal caused him so much anxiety that he simply took home whatever broken appliance he came across to avoid feeling it. The regret in passing up an item or getting rid of broken appliances, as Jason imagined it, was overwhelming and crippling, not momentary and manageable. Walking around his house with him, I saw that most of the appliances, from my perspective, would not have been those that others would have wanted.

Jason could not see this, however. He saw value in the satisfaction he expected to experience in fixing them and giving them as gifts.

The excitement in Jason's eyes while he relived how he acquired his finds, how little they cost, and whom he intended to give them to reminded me of how a drug addict lights up at the thought of a score. When he talked to me, it was clear that adrenaline had taken over, and adrenaline likely ruled him during his acquiring sprees. In the several sessions I later had with him in my office, he did not betray the same level of excitement and energy that he had in that moment, which led me to conclude that Jason was strongly compelled by the pleasurable feelings of being near the objects and acquiring them. Some people who hoard are driven more strongly by the need to acquire than others. Some, like Joan, who didn't go out on gathering or shopping sprees, are more plagued by the inability to get rid of things, rather than a drive to go out and forage.

To encourage Jason to question his cognitive distortions, in a non-judgmental tone, I asked him if it was his belief that the coffeemaker sitting in front of me would be of value to someone else, even though it had no coffeepot. He said yes, because perhaps he might be able to find a pot, or the person he intended to give it to might have one. I then asked him to rate his anxiety level on a scale of 0 to 10 if he had to let go of the coffeemaker, so we could experiment to see if his prediction of what he would feel was accurate.

This process of encouraging a patient to practice letting go of valued objects and sitting with the stress and anxiety is called expo-sure, and it's a primary component of treating compulsive hoarding. I will ask a client to rate the amount of anxiety he feels at the thought of giving up an item, and then, when he does give up the item, ask him whether he feels as bad as he thought he would. Far more often than not, he finds that his prediction of how much anxiety he'd feel was far worse than what he actually felt, and in so doing, he learns that he can handle parting with the things he doesn't need. It's a process—it's not as if a compulsive hoarder does it once and from then on has no problem discarding his hoarded items—but with practice, it becomes easier and represents real progress. Chapter 5 contains much more on exposure.

Jason, however, reported that the anxiety he experienced at giving up the coffeemaker was an 8 out of 10. This was too high a level for me to ask him to part with it, so we walked around looking for another item that might represent a 2- or 3-level range of anxiety. But we never found it. Nothing was below a 7.

I realized I had to continue to work with Jason on his cognitive distortions about the perceived value of the items. These cognitive distortions allowed him to avoid the anxiety he feared he would feel if he passed up what he perceived as a fantastic deal and someone did, in fact, need the rehabbed appliance. He believed he would never be able to forgive himself if this happened. People with anxiety disorders such as compulsive hoarding suffer from distorted thinking about the future, and many fear they will never get over the regret of letting go of a particular item.

Bringing the World into Your Home

When people like Jason—who have an overwhelming urge to acquire— bring home their latest acquisitions, they have great difficulty making decisions about how to incorporate the items into their home. Even if they find they have no use for them, they want to hold on, because they "never know" if it will come in handy one day.

I'm often asked where the line is drawn between what's "normal" in terms of acquiring and clutter, and what is compulsive hoarding. Many people who do not suffer from compulsive hoarding do have what we call hoarding tendencies, or behaviors that are common among people who hoard. For example, a person might be unable to resist a "deal" and thus acquires too much, but is not disorganized and the person does not become overly attached to too many things. Occasionally I'll see strong tendencies in children or teenagers, and know that those tendencies are at risk of blossoming into a more severe hoarding condition during adulthood if they aren't addressed. Typically someone is in compulsive hoarding territory when his ability to function is impaired by his relationship to his stuff, and his stuff is taking over the living environment.

To an extent, that line is subjective, and unfortunately, many with this condition lack the ability to see or acknowledge that their lives are, in fact, impaired by the way they live, even if it's exceedingly clear to their loved ones. Melissa, whom I mentioned in Chapter 1, lived in a thoroughly hoarded home with her husband, Barry. Their relationship had grown distant, and they argued frequently over the state of their home, which in itself can be a sign that things are out of control. Still, when I asked Melissa what she thought of the state of her home, she described it as "a bit cluttered."

RETAIL THERAPY TO SOLVE ANY PROBLEM

Added to the struggle many of us, hoarders and non-hoarders alike, have with keeping our lives organized and free of clutter is the perception that the answers to many of our problems are available at the local mall, on sale, while supplies last. Shopping is a fun, soothing, social activity for many of us. (I personally love to shop, especially with my mother—it's a way of bonding for us.) Ubiquitous advertising and marketing messages lead us to believe that handy items or fabulous luxuries can instantly improve our lives: There's nothing that can't be solved by purchasing the right item or the newest gadget. You were doing just fine with your computer . . . until you saw the new iPad, and all of a sudden, you have a new thing to want, even though your needs haven't changed. Given how much the average person is affected by this messaging, imagine viewing the endless montage of advertising through the eyes of someone who has a particularly distorted view of what material possessions can and cannot do for them.

Many people who struggle with hoarding acquire and shop to try to deal with emotions that they don't otherwise know how to manage.

I once worked with a woman in her late twenties, Amanda, who lived with her parents and spent her days watching the Home Shopping Network, while at the same time surfing the Internet for good deals. Her parents were fairly wealthy and did not require Amanda to work or for the most part engage in any activities during the day. Mind you, it wasn't that they didn't *hope* that she might pursue an educational or occupational endeavor, but they didn't press the issue. So Amanda would spend her days cooped up in her room, completely isolated from others, in her shopping frenzy. Part of the thrill for her was the ring of the doorbell. Amanda would fly down the stairs, often skipping steps, as if Santa Claus had just come in on his sleigh to deliver her gifts. "I'll get it!" she would yell, running to greet the UPS or Federal Express driver. Once she had her treasure, she would run upstairs to slam the door and tear open her newest purchase.

As soon as her purchase was unwrapped, however, she'd leave it where it landed, and there it sat. Amanda would immediately turn back to surfing the Internet. This behavior went on until she was 27 and her parents called me for a consultation. Their house was becoming smaller and smaller; the hallways and upstairs rooms were filled with boxes. I encouraged them to set boundaries with Amanda, place financial limits on her, and express their expectations for her continued residence in their home. They tried, but Amanda just couldn't seem to follow through on these rules. Ultimately, she agreed to see me herself.

It took only one home visit with Amanda for me to get a sense of her condition. She began to come into my office for therapy over the next several months. We talked about how her shopping was an empty and ineffective attempt to solve her bigger problem, which was loneliness. Uncomfortable in social situations, Amanda found that shopping gave her something to do and a sense of a connection to the outside world. Acquiring things she thought she wanted was, for her, a substitute for meaningful human interaction—something she craved but didn't know how to achieve. We talked about ways that she could begin to reintegrate herself into the community and let go of her compulsive shopping as a means of connecting with the world at large. She was able to commit to getting rid of items that were returnable, and use the refunded money to begin attending college classes. Those items that she could not return were sold at multiple garage sales at her parents' home. After months of treatment and diligent at-home follow-up, Amanda shared the realization that she was hoping her stuff would make her feel happier, and admitted that she'd been living a very lonely existence.

NON-HOARDERS WITH HOARDING TENDENCIES

Everyone has a tough time parting with his or her possessions to some degree. What distinguishes people who hoard from non-hoarders is just how difficult they find it, and how many items the person has difficulty parting with. Many non-hoarders regularly toss unnecessary items, clean out closets, and donate or make gifts of things they no longer have any use for. Not engaging in these kinds of cleaning and purging activities often enough to keep your home free of clutter—to the point that it makes a storage space or room unusable—is a hoarding tendency.

My friend Alexa recently helped her mother clean out the home she lived in with Alexa's stepfather, Robert, after he passed away. The house always looked tidy—Alexa's mother is a neat person who isn't particularly sentimental about material things—but there were several rooms that had been her stepfather's domain. There, Alexa and her mom discovered piles and drawers full of papers, maps, ticket stubs, and matchbooks from trips taken before she and Robert were married, warranties for appliances long since replaced, and loads of artwork from his now-grown children. They found unused ceramic mugs from public relations events he'd attended in the course of his work (they were at least 20 years old, since he had retired long before he died), cheap canvas tote bags with corporate logos of companies he'd worked

DO YOU HAVE HOARDING TENDENCIES?

The following are tendencies that are very common in those who struggle with hoarding, and to a lesser extent in non-hoarders. Read the questions below and note how many of these feelings resonate with you.

1. Do you have a hard time parting with items, even if you never use them or they're broken?

2. Do you have many items around your house that don't have a permanent home?

3. Do you tend to make piles of things, to be dealt with at a future time, and these piles often linger for more than a few days?

4. Are there areas in your home (the dining room table, for instance) that must be cleared off before they can be used for their intended purpose?

5. Do you save things often because you are concerned about how you will feel if you need them in the future and no longer have them?

6. Do you often save things without a clear idea of how you'll use them in the future?

with over the years, and old cameras for which film was no longer made. They found piles of unused office supplies and envelopes so old the adhesive had dried up. There were caches of liquor, unopened bottles of wine and spirits that he'd received as gifts, which he'd stashed away with the intent of using for entertaining one day, because Robert himself didn't drink. The amount of stuff was staggering, and none of it had been used for years.

Robert would not be characterized as someone who hoards, because his stuff didn't interfere with his life, and his house was not a mess. But like many of us, he had hoarding tendencies, along with a large house with lots of nooks and crannies, and a lifetime to fill it up. He saw no need to throw away anything—as long as there was room

7. Do you still have items that you once bought with the intention of giving them away as gifts?

8. Do you have boxes of possessions that have moved with you from home to home but you've never gone through?

9. Do you often buy multiples of the same item because you've forgotten you have it?

10. Are you helpless when faced with a "good deal," even if it's a good deal on something you don't need?

11. Do you take free things, like shampoos from hotels or packets of soup crackers, that you never wind up using?

The more of these questions you answered yes to, the stronger your hoarding tendencies, and your environment is likely cluttered accordingly. If you answered yes to all of them, it does not mean you are a hoarder; many of us have hoarding tendencies, but because they are kept in check, things don't escalate to the point where your life is greatly affected. Still, the more you have, the more mindful you need to be of your habits so your environment does not cause you undue stress.

for an object, why should he? Like many people, when faced with something for which he had no immediate use, he would keep it, just in case it could prove useful one day.

When Alexa was cleaning up, she came across a large ball made of rubber bands, which she felt was symbolic of Robert's hoarding tendencies. Robert never used more than one or two of the rubber bands he took off his morning newspaper, but would fish them out of the trash if he saw that Alexa's mom had thrown one away, and add them to the ball. While his grandchildren did, in fact, get a kick out of the rubber band ball a couple of times when they visited, he kept it long after they'd lost interest, "just in case" they decided they wanted to play with it again.

Like the vast majority of us, Robert preferred to do other things with his time than sort through his stuff. Even though there was nothing unusual about Robert's relationship to his possessions, when he died, his wife was able to fill up a 22-foot-long Dumpster with trash and donate truckloads more. It was particularly poignant for Alexa and her mother to see what he saved, because much of it was filled with intent—something I see constantly among people who suffer from this condition. Robert is a classic example of someone who had strong hoarding tendencies.

WHY WE SAVE WHAT WE SAVE

Like most of us, Robert saw his possessions as special—they meant something to him, even if that meaning wasn't apparent to others. This emotional quality is what gives our stuff so much power in our lives, and what can make it so hard to keep our lives free of clutter.

Our possessions can represent a variety of things to us. Following are a few of the most common connotations we associate with the things in our lives.

MEMORIES, BOTH POSITIVE AND NEGATIVE. Perhaps you have a collection of sea glass from a trip to the shore when you were a child, and looking at the worn-down aqua and green shards reminds you of a happy beach vacation. Or maybe you have an old concert T-shirt that is stained and no longer fits, but it feels important to keep because it was purchased on one of the best nights of your life. For many years, Diana, 42, kept a coat she had never worn, because her husband bought it for her on their honeymoon in Paris. "It was white and made of velvet, but I never wore it because we had young children and it would have been dirty in no time. It was totally impractical, but the fact that he bought it for me and thought I would love it made me think about how much he wanted to please me back then."

When Diana and her husband split up, she finally donated the coat to charity because it became a reminder of all the potential that was once in her marriage, and it made her sad. But some people keep things that bring up sad memories, precisely because they feel it's important to remember the negative feelings the items represent. Robbie, who is 53, still keeps a videotape of a self-defense class that she took after being sexually assaulted in her early thirties. She never watches the tape. In fact, she doesn't even own a VCR anymore—just a DVD player. But, she says, "I feel like it's a reminder of what I went through, and remembering that makes me see how far I've come. It doesn't make me feel good, exactly, but it feels important to keep." Many, many people purchased gold coins and other objects commemorating the events of 9/11. There's nothing wrong with keeping mementos of a tragic event, but when the items are of no use, make a person feel bad, and contribute to clutter, I would argue they should not be kept or collected.

Challenge Yourself and Take Action: Do you have a stash of items you've been holding on to because of the powerful memories (positive or negative) that you associate with them? As you sort through these items and hold each one, ask yourself: Does it evoke good feelings (warm, happy, proud, excited, for example) or does seeing it and touching it make you feel bad (guilty, remiss, regretful, or chastened)? If an item doesn't make you feel good, it's okay to get rid of it. If you have a problem with clutter, you might consider getting rid of an item even if it does make you feel good. It's a matter of prioritizing what you keep and not holding on to every single tennis trophy you've ever earned. I suggest creating a small, manageable memento box, or keeping only one symbol of a triumph or positive memory. After her marriage broke up, Diana went through her teeming box of photographs and got rid of the ones that evoked a negative memory, which motivated her to make an album out of the ones that remained, rather than ignoring the box and hoping they'd organize themselves.

ERAS OF OUR LIVES. Alexa keeps two dozen philosophy books from college, even though she hasn't read them in 20 years and her work today has nothing to do with the subject matter, so she likely will never have any use for them again. "I work so hard now, and life is so stressful. I like what I do, but it's all about responsibility," she says. "Those books remind me of a time when I had the time to think about bigger, impractical issues."

It's fine to keep a few items that represent a happy era of your life, but if you're concerned about clutter, it's a matter of being selective. Picking out the books from the courses she most enjoyed, perhaps 10 or 12, and displaying them prominently on a shelf would cut back on clutter while reminding her of the positive memories associated with them. Alexa's need to maintain a connection with the intellectual curiosity of her college days is harmless; but sometimes we hold on to items from our past in order to teach ourselves a lesson, which may not be healthy. Many of us were raised to believe that guilt and self-punishment are motivational, but they are generally not effective motivators, and in fact can be quite self-defeating. Carol, a 43-year-old producer whom I have worked with in the past, keeps several large boxes in her garage that are filled with photos from two failed marriages. When I asked her why she doesn't get rid of the pictures (or pare them down so as to keep only a few), she said, "It's a piece of my history. If I let go of them, I may be giving up some of my history. I learned a lot in my first marriage. If I give up the pictures, does it make me less accountable to what I've learned?"

The desire to keep an object that helps you remember a hard-earned lesson sounds like a good reason for keeping it, but it's important to consider how that item is really serving you. Carol told me that she still feels guilty about leaving her first husband, and seeing those boxes didn't make her feel like she'd gained wisdom and grown as a person. Instead, every time she saw them, she beat herself up for having hurt someone she cared about. Carol also admitted that on some level she thinks her ex-husband's feelings would be hurt if she tossed the pictures, even though they're not in touch, so he'd never know. While the boxes do not pose any kind of a hazard and her home is organized and neat, seeing them every time she parks her car may be preventing Carol from moving on emotionally with her life. The boxes serve as a constant reminder that she cannot go back and undo past mistakes.

Challenge Yourself and Take Action: Are you holding on to objects that you never use because you'd feel guilty or that you're a bad person if you threw them away? This is a thought distortion, a belief about what your stuff says about you that is not only untrue, but serves to keep you surrounded by clutter, and what's more, clutter that makes you feel bad, not good, about yourself. The truth is, what you keep has nothing to do with what kind of person you are. Ask yourself if the items you're holding on to really help keep you from repeating past mistakes, or if they simply remind you of them.

OUR PAST SELVES. Carla, a new mom at 28, is unable to part with a pair of high-heeled sandals that she could barely wear when she first got them 9 years ago, when she was single and dated near the army base where she met her now-husband. There's no harm in her keeping them, because they don't take up much room and she doesn't have an especially cluttered home, but Carla realizes she'll never wear them again. "Except maybe as part of a Halloween costume," she jokes. "I'm not that person anymore."

Those shoes make Carla smile when she looks at them, and perhaps on some level Carla keeps them because she likes to believe she can tap into that part of herself again or go back in time when motherhood gets a bit overwhelming. But just as with saving things that remind us of negative experiences in our past, some people save things that remind them of people that they no longer are, and are relieved to have left behind.

Tara, a 42-year-old graduate student, underwent a horrible trauma when she was 13: She was in a fire, which caused terrible scarring. Her adolescence was very difficult because she was in the hospital a lot, and the scarring affected her confidence in her appearance. It took her almost 2 decades to get over the physical and emotional trauma.

When she tells me about this, Tara refers to the various stages of her recovery as if she had been a different person during each phase, and of the books, clothing, and pictures that were important to these various women as "they" were going through their struggles. "I feel that I need to hold on to these things, because it would be dishonoring the person I was at the time when I needed them if I didn't." Tara says that these items give her a sense of validation for the struggles her past selves experienced, even though they do not produce positive memories today. At the end of our work together, Tara was able to recognize the many thinking errors, or cognitive distortions, that were leading her to keep these items and that she was not letting go of any part of herself in letting go of the possessions. It didn't happen overnight, but eventually, she was able to part with many of these objects.

Challenge Yourself and Take Action: Does a particular item from your past make you remember the person you once were, and invoke happy or proud feelings? If so, and it's small and is not one of many that are contributing to the clutter in your home, keep it. But if it's one of many such items, and especially if it keeps you ruminating over past life traumas, consider letting it go. You do not need to keep the item in order to be proud of whom you have become. In Tara's case, I talked with her about how that person who struggled through such hard times helped her become the strong person she is today, and that she didn't need the stuff to remember that. She found that realization enormously freeing, and was able to get rid of many of these objects.

ASPIRATIONS. People often purchase status symbol items (or status symbol knockoffs), such as designer handbags, shoes, sunglasses, or other objects we carry with us every day. Even if we can't quite afford them, these objects communicate a certain status and value to those around us: This is the kind of person we'd like to be. Susan, a mom of two and a substance abuse counselor, hasn't worked in 2 years, yet continues to acquire the latest laptops, sunglasses, and handbags, and drives a car she can ill afford, justifying it by saying that she needs to look well put together to get another job. But in an attempt to maintain a certain image, she is spending money she doesn't have, and accumulating clutter.

For Susan, it's the *possibility* of being the person who could afford these items that is so valuable to her, and that's what the items have come to represent. If she were to throw them away, she fears all that potential and optimism would go out with them.

Challenge Yourself and Take Action: Does having all that high-end stuff really move you closer to your goals, or is it more of a temporary feel-good fix when you acquire them? The truth is, looking the part of wealthy and successful only leads you to spend money you don't have and adds to your clutter and sense of regret when the bills come. To an extent, presentation is important, and we all want to feel proud of our appearance. But status symbols are just that—symbols, not status itself. It would be more emotionally gratifying to focus on what you want to do and be, rather than looking the part.

PEOPLE WHO ARE NO LONGER WITH US. It's not uncommon to save a book or a piece of jewelry because it once belonged to a loved one. Photos of relatives who have passed away, of course, help us remember them, and seeing these pictures can evoke happy memories. Denise, a 46-year-old real estate broker who was a client of mine, had a home cluttered with children's toys. Denise's children were grown and had moved out of the house years ago. While her kids are not gone from this Earth, their childhoods are, and Denise needed to work on understanding that the memories of those times were not only living in the objects, but in her heart as well. Learning to let go of some of the stuff in her home would help her to move on emotionally and also grow by experiencing new things and making new memories that she could cherish.

In fact, saving things in the memory of a loved one can greatly impair the lives of the living. Bill, the police officer whose daughter was killed by a drunk driver, held on to her clothing and childhood mementos, because in his grief he couldn't bring himself to sort through them. Much of her stuff became moldy in his basement, where rats ate it and excreted on it. Still, he believed that his daughter's clothing somehow contained the essence of her, and that was why it was so hard to get rid of it. While holding on to some of his daughter's stuff would not have been a problem, his hoarding was about avoiding working through the grief over his daughter's death. The more he avoided that, the worse his hoarding became, making his loss even more powerful and disabling. In short, living in the past prevented him from embracing his present, one that he found too painful to deal with.

Challenge Yourself and Take Action: Are you memorializing your loved ones in a meaningful way, or might there be a more fitting means of honoring their memory, such as a charitable donation made in their name, or keeping one small item rather than many? These people who were once in our lives would likely be proud of you for making good decisions about your living environment and your emotional health. Consider picking one item from the person who is gone, and display it in a meaningful way. If your relationship with that person was a difficult one, and seeing the item reminds you of that and brings up unpleasant emotions, don't keep the item where you will see it every day, but rather someplace where you can access it if you want to. If while decluttering you find that there is room to keep more than one item, that's great. But remember, your loved one would probably feel most honored if the item is treated respectfully and is kept where it can be appreciated, rather than in the midst of clutter or at the bottom of a pile.

PERIODS OF DEARTH. I grew up in an affluent neighborhood, but our family didn't have the kind of money that our neighbors did—I was the girl in the high-water pants. I can't tell you how many times I heard, "Waiting for a flood, Robin?" Everyone else had the designer jeans, and now, perhaps partially because of this, I like clothes and I love to shop. I do my best to not bring clothes into the house unless I'm prepared to get rid of an equal amount of stuff, so my closet doesn't get too crowded, but I definitely feel some comfort in having more than I strictly need.

The problem arises when the fear of doing without leads to the accumulation of far more than anyone could possibly use. This was the case with my patient Dominique, a fashion designer mom of three. After her divorce, Dominique was very worried about money, so she saved everything for a future time in which she feared she'd have no money to buy things. She also shopped, spending her child support check on clothing, both because she enjoyed it and to relieve her anxiety. She

wound up in a hoarded house and was at risk of losing the most important thing in her life: her daughters.

Similarly, Alexa's grandfather William had closets full of clothing
that he no longer wore and even kept a case of soap that he'd bought
that irritated his skin and he could never use. It felt wasteful to throw
any of this out, because as a child of the Great Depression, he acutely
remembered what it was like to do without. Like Robert, he died with
a closet full of items he didn't need.

Challenge Yourself and Take Action: Are you shopping to excess
to make up for the fact that you didn't have all of the things you wanted
or needed earlier in your life, or are you driven by the fear that you
might not have what you need in the future? If so, ask yourself whether
the item you are considering purchasing is truly going to resolve either
problem. The answer is probably no, but if you're not sure, take an
inventory of what you already have and are using and not using.
Remember, an item isn't a "good deal" if you don't have any use for
it now or in the near future. Consider that purchasing things you
don't need out of a desire to avoid a situation in which you don't have
what you want actually costs you money and ironically makes you less
able to provide the things you do need for yourself.

ACHIEVEMENTS. A few years ago, I worked with a little boy who
suffered from anxiety. His room was quite messy, and he was beginning to show signs of having a problem with clutter. I asked him what
things he had a hard time parting with, and he showed me a notebook
from two grades prior that was so tattered that the cardboard had
worn through the outside covering. He shared that he had liked his
teacher that year and earned the best grades in her class that he's ever
received—he didn't want to forget her. He told me that he was scared
that if he threw away the notebook, it would mean that he didn't care
about the teacher who had helped him be the best he could be, and that

he would be literally throwing away his achievement. I acknowledged his feelings and validated his concerns, but challenged that his achievement would not be thrown out with the notebook. I gave him an example of an Olympic gold medalist: If he lost his medal, did that mean he didn't win the race? By pointing out the distortion in his thinking, I was able to help him understand that letting the item go didn't diminish his accomplishments.

Challenge Yourself and Take Action: Will getting rid of an item that reminds you of a great feat you once achieved diminish your accomplishments? Probably not. Your life experiences are yours, regardless of whether you have a physical reminder of what you've achieved. If the item is old, damaged, or doesn't have great meaning to you anymore, it's reasonable to toss it. The symbols of your achievements—trophies, medals, thank-you notes—are reasonable for you to keep depending on how much you have. If you're having a problem with clutter, picking one or two, or making a scrapbook of articles about yourself, rather than keeping many, can be helpful in maintaining a neat environment.

PUNISHMENT. I know a man who has a case full of football trophies from high school, where he was a star lineman on the varsity team. Now, he is overweight and only plays football occasionally on the weekends, but he keeps those trophies to remind himself that he needs to get back in shape. Women (like Kate, who you may remember kept clothing that was two sizes too small for her) often do the same thing. They keep a pair of jeans they fit into 10 years ago or a dress they wore in college because they think these items will motivate them to get back in shape. They believe they should have to look at these relics from their past as a form of self-punishment for gaining weight and being unable to lose it.

Carol, the woman who keeps boxes of photos from her marriages in the garage, saves the photos from her second marriage to teach herself a lesson. Her second husband was a grifter. He seemed to have it all together and passed himself off as wildly successful, but in reality he was unemployed and took her money and left. Carol had an inkling that something wasn't right during their whirlwind courtship, but pushed aside her doubts because she was in love. "His leaving was a gift, but it was horribly upsetting at the time. I don't want to make the same mistakes again, and I think keeping the pictures will keep me accountable," she says. She believes that looking at those boxes (she never looks at the pictures themselves) reminds her that she needs to listen to her instincts.

I'm not so sure. It seems like self-punishment to me, and negative motivators and self-flagellation don't typically help people make positive changes. Sometimes when I'm helping a client sort through his possessions, I'll inquire about the value or relevance of a particular item. After a bit more questioning, it becomes clear that he is keeping it not because he likes it or uses it, but because he spent money on it and now regrets it. Keeping it, he'll say, is a reminder not to waste money on foolish purchases. "I was foolish to buy it in the first place" is typical of self-punishing talk. When I ask if it's helpful to be reminded of being "foolish," the answer is usually no.

Challenge Yourself and Take Action: Are you keeping a particular item or items because you think seeing it will make you feel bad enough about yourself that you'll change your behavior? If so, toss it. Negative motivation usually doesn't work, even though it's very common for parents to try to motivate children this way, especially if that was the way they were once raised. Imagine you were an employer, and you had an employee who you hoped would do a better job. Would you encourage the employee by nitpicking his work and insulting his intelligence, or by praising his work and pointing out how he can improve his performance? The same goes when "talking" to yourself about your past, in this case through what reminders you choose to keep around. You will likely get much better results and feel less defeated if you focus on your past successes rather than ways in which you didn't do well.

POSSIBILITY IN GENERAL. Several years ago I helped a woman named Donna, who had a very full life. She had three children and six grandchildren; worked a 40-hour-a-week job; and babysat her grandchildren many nights a week. Donna's house was overflowing with materials for craft projects that she had every intention of tackling. There was yarn for needlepoint, papers for scrapbooking, and various materials for painting and home repair projects—none of which were ever completed. Still, on the weekends when she had time to shop, she would frequently find herself in one of her favorite craft stores, "just to look around and see if there might be some good deals." Of course there were good deals. There will always be good deals. I believe these craft materials represented the possibility that she would eventually have time to do these activities, and that sense of optimism made her feel good.

But Donna would bring home the bags of recently purchased craft supplies and set them on the floor in the dining room, the living room, and the spare bedroom, all of which were so full that you could barely enter the rooms. She never put away the supplies (her home was so crowded there was no obvious place to put them), and so there they sat. Her husband had given up on asking her what she bought. He felt it was a losing battle, and his questions always turned into arguments, as she would rationalize her good intentions. This time, she was always certain, the project would get completed. For the previous 4 years, their house had been perpetually decorated for Christmas, because even the project of taking down the decorations was never completed. The craft room and surrounding areas contained decorations for July 4th, Thanksgiving, Easter, and all the other major holidays. There were stacks, bags, and boxes of holiday items, none of which had ever been used, but she kept buying more because she couldn't resist an after-holiday sale. Donna's good intentions led her nowhere except to a cluttered home and a tense marriage.

Challenge Yourself and Take Action: Do you have a stockpile of items (possibly in your garage or your basement) that you bought with the intention of using them for a home improvement project that was never seen through to the end? Are you realistically going to have a use for these items in the foreseeable future? If not, consider donating or tossing them. The worst thing that will happen is that you'll have to buy what you need again when you do have time to execute your good intentions. But once you get rid of it, you'll realize that you can live with the tiny risk that you may need one of those items at some point in the future. The price of a clutter-free home and mind is likely to outweigh the price of the item itself.

SECURITY. Having more than they need of something can make many people feel secure. For example, you might think, "If I buy my favorite shampoo every time it's on sale, I'll never have to worry about running out of it some morning." And before you know it, your bathroom cabinets are so packed with bottles of shampoo that there's no room for your other toiletries.

Michael, 62, an insurance broker, grew up in a large family. Often when he was counting on eating something, he'd arrive home to find that one of his siblings had beaten him to it. "To this day, even though I only live with my wife, who doesn't eat that much, I'll buy more food than we need," he laughs. Michael will buy four cans of soup or boxes of pasta, instead of one or two. "My wife jokes that we could open a soup kitchen, and she has a point, but I like the feeling of knowing that the food I want will be there when I get home." Michael usually overstocks food, but he has also been known to store paper towels, toilet paper, shampoo, shaving cream, and razors—all the necessities. In other words, while food was the only thing he worried about running out of when he was a child, his fears of doing without spread into other areas of his life as well.

People who hoard food or other staples don't always do so because of an experience of deprivation at some earlier point in their lives. The thrill of the deal can also trigger it—offers like "buy two, get one free," or "buy this product and save 50 percent on another product" (often a product you don't even need). People who have trouble resisting a good deal have an especially difficult time making good purchasing decisions at warehouse stores like Costco, which are founded on the principle that buying in quantity gets you the better deal. Everyone likes a good deal.

The problem, of course, is that it's easy to buy more than you need and clutter your home with these items. When you stockpile food, you're unlikely to be organized enough to know what you already have and what you need, so you simply go buy more of the same items. This obviously becomes particularly problematic with food that has a short expiration date. It's not uncommon for individuals who have a problem with hoarding food to have trouble throwing it away even after it's expired—because in their minds, there still might be use for it. People who hoard food will often suggest that expiration dates are arbitrarily set by manufacturers to get us to buy more food, and reason that throwing away any food is wasteful. Yet they will not eat the expired food, and they continue to buy more. I have worked with countless people who have kept rotten bananas with the expressed intent to eat them, milk from more than 3 years ago, and canned food older than a decade.

Tara, the woman who spent time in the hospital as a child after being burned in a fire and saved things from her "past selves," confessed to me that she had a loaf of bread that she'd baked 3 years earlier in her freezer. When she was a child, she had a very delicate stomach, and there were few foods she could tolerate, so she was very careful to keep on hand those foods she could eat. Now she can eat whatever she'd like, but she still has a hard time letting go of that loaf of bread.

When we talked about it, Tara laughed and said she understood that it was not rational to save 3-year-old bread, and at one point she tried a bite and expressed that it tasted "like freezer." But she thought if she held on to it, she could use it to make breadcrumbs one day. Ultimately, we talked it through—she could make more bread if she needed to, and this bread tasted bad, so it was unlikely she was going to make bread-crumbs out of it—and she eventually threw away the freezer-burned bread. It took Tara playing out all the scenarios in her head of what would happen if she found herself without bread when she needed it to realize that as an adult (not a sick child dependent on others for food), she could handle it.

Challenge Yourself and Take Action: Do you keep more food than you need in your home? Are you unable to resist a good deal at the grocery store and, as a result, find that you have more cans of soup or boxes of cereal than you know what to do with? When someone is keeping more food than they can possibly eat, I encourage them to go through their refrigerator, pantry, cupboards, and any other storage areas and start with purging all items that are expired. Don't rationalize that it still may be good! You cannot donate expired food to feed the hungry—food banks will not accept it. If that's the case, you shouldn't eat it either. Next, start thinking of recipes for meals using what you have. And from now on, try to refrain from going shopping without taking an inventory of what you have and making a list. Be careful not to get caught up in special deals and sales. Buy only what you need.

WHAT YOUR STUFF SAYS ABOUT YOU

Of course, any item can be symbolic, but that doesn't necessarily mean every item you keep is symbolic of something meaningful in your life.

For instance, people who have an issue with clutter might keep dozens of pens simply because they work, and might be needed in the future, although they are not terribly hard to come by and nobody needs more than a few at a time. I have noticed some trends in the kinds of objects that people tend to keep and have some reluctance to throw away. Here are a number of common items that create clutter in people's homes.

- **Books:** So many people compulsively hoard books that there is a separate word for it: *bibliomania.* Whether the number of books you have constitutes bibliomania or simply a love of books (*bibliophilia,* which is not a psychological disorder) depends on the number and type of books you own, as well as the context of your living situation. Joan, whose books had taken over her house and had been destroyed by her cats, had a need for books that went beyond the simple enjoyment of reading or collecting them. They were a liability in her home and prevented her from living in a healthy environment, because they were piled high on the floor and in double rows on her bookshelf. She had bagfuls of books, and her many cats had urinated on some of them.

   Books convey a positive symbolism for most of us. Like they did for Alexa, books can represent a period in our lives when we had more time to read and think, and many people like to keep books because they represent knowledge and information at their fingertips, or they believe they make a home look as if a smart, well-informed person is living there. Not being able to get rid of books, even when there are way too many, often has to do with being afraid of not having immediate access to the information they contain.

- **Periodicals:** Many people who hoard keep stacks and stacks of magazines and newspapers that become moldy or moist and can cause a health hazard. Most say that they plan to get around to reading them at some point, but when pressed, others say fascinating things about why they hold on to them: Some say that they feel they're keeping the memory of the time the publication was printed (the memory, of course, is in them, not in the periodical). Others have said that a newspaper represents the work of so many people that throwing it away feels unkind to those who worked so hard to produce it. Most non-hoarders save publications because there's something in the magazine or newspaper that they want to use or reference again, such as a recipe they want to make or a review of a book they want to remember to purchase.

• **E-mails, texts, and voicemails:** Cyberhoarding is a new phenomenon I've observed, especially among people who do not have any other problems with clutter. One client of mine, Steven, who came to my clinic for multiple anxiety issues including OCD and social phobia, is a 25-year-old college student from a very dysfunctional family. His parents exhibited a lot of hostility and unpredictable behavior over the years, which caused him great anxiety.

When I was first getting to know Steven, I called him a few times to follow up on appointments and noticed that each time I did, his voicemail box was full. I asked him about this, and he explained that he had retained messages from his high school years (he had graduated years before) on his phone, as well as messages from family members. When I asked Steven why he couldn't erase the messages, he said that high school was the best time in his life, and he feared he would forget the memories if he erased the messages. He also said that because of his anxiety issues, he had not experienced any happy memories for the past few years and feared he may never have any in the future. He held on to his family members' positive messages for the same reason: "What if they never send me one again?" Ironically, saving those messages meant that Steven couldn't get any new messages, which defeated the purpose of having voicemail at the very least, and at worst, interfered with his ability to make new friends and live up to his current responsibilities. Steven's cyberhoarding, even though it didn't take up physical space, still compromised his ability to function in a healthy way. He saved texts as well.

E-mail hoarding is much more common than one might imagine. Sandy, 22, a freelance graphic designer, recently had to open up a new e-mail account because her mailbox was at 100 percent capacity. She couldn't bring herself to delete any of her old e-mails, even some from 4 years back. Sandy worried that she might need the details of a conversation, and if she cleaned out her inbox, that information would be lost forever. She knew there were many that could go, but she was so afraid that she'd permanently delete the wrong one and then regret it, and that doing so might lead to loss of income or important contact information if she couldn't lay her hands on the conversations she needed. What's more, to take the time to read through the 10,000 e-mails in her inbox just seemed too daunting—Sandy knew she should have done it when there were fewer, but by the time there were so many, she was completely overwhelmed at the prospect. It is much easier to put it off, and in Sandy's case, never get to it. Opening the new account was not difficult, but it was confusing to her clients, who couldn't find her easily.

• **Records, bank statements, and paperwork:** Many people have trouble keeping their paperwork under control, and oftentimes it can be even worse for those who work at home. Joy, who is 53 and runs a stock photography agency out of her otherwise tidy home, has dozens of boxes of images and paperwork from decades past. "Every time I try to get rid of them, I think someone might call for a certain picture, and I will regret having gotten rid of it and then it will cost me money," she says. Saving thousands of files in case one person calls for a photo is excessive, which Joy recognizes. Still, she keeps them.

I believe the main reason the average person holds on to this kind of clutter is because most people simply do not know what to keep and what to toss—how long do you need to save bank statements, for instance? How far back might the IRS audit you? If there is symbolism buried in these piles, it might be that keeping this stuff is symbolic of being responsible, even though the reality is, it's hard to find what you need when you need it because of the mess. (Turn to Chapter 7 for more information on what items you need to keep and for how long.)

• **Shoes, handbags, and clothing:** I think that shoes and bags, for women, anyway, represent options, and it's nice to feel like you have options, not to mention the fact that shoes usually still fit even when other things don't anymore. Keeping clothes that no longer fit with the idea that they might one day fit again may represent hope. Perhaps if you've lost a lot of weight and keep your larger clothes, it's a reminder not to go there again, or permission, on some level, to put the weight back on.

Some women express themselves creatively with their clothes, and so like to keep more than they need, and for some, like Anita, a 25-year-old nonprofit administrator who lives with roommates, it's like a mini museum of their lives. "I'm afraid to let go of my clothes—it's like an identity thing," Anita says. "The clothes represent different times of my life." She keeps her cheerleading T-shirt from high school, crew shirts from college, casual clothes and professional clothes ("These two identities conflict with one another, but they are also both me," she says), and "hippie" clothes she likes wearing to concerts. "All those different forms of clothing make up who I am as a person, and I like to have all these parts."

If you have enough room for all of your clothes, terrific. But if, like Anita, you're tight on space and cannot keep your things organized, consider cleaning out your closet and getting rid of the items you no longer need. You can still be proud of the various parts of your personality and your life without keeping the wardrobe that goes along with them.

• **Jewelry:** An engagement ring symbolizes a promise or a commitment, and "push jewelry," such as a necklace your husband gave you when you had your first child, is a symbol of his appreciation for what you went through and are building together. Jewelry, of course, can also be a symbol of wealth. While jewelry doesn't take up much space, and isn't a major source of clutter for most people, many non-hoarders have a box that contains earrings they hope to one day find the mates to, broken jewelry that they mean to get repaired, or items that were given to them but that they will likely never wear.

• **Children's things:** Parents whose kids have grown up often are more attached to their kids' toys and clothes than the kids themselves ever were. It can represent a simpler time, before big children meant big problems, or simply a love of having been a parent. It's fine to keep a small item—a favorite doll or truck—to show your grandchildren, but keeping too many toys or clothes that no one is using will only add to your clutter.

A FORTRESS OF CLUTTER

For most of this chapter, we've focused on the symbolic meaning of common items, and the feelings—both positive and negative—that we associate with them. But some people also find comfort, or at least familiarity, in the amount of their belongings rather than the quality of them. It is the sheer physical nature of the clutter, as opposed to what the clutter is comprised of, that makes it hard for them to let it go.

One of the reasons is that physical clutter can feel protective, like a fortress of stuff. While of course too many things don't literally prevent people from getting close, it can be protective in an emotional sense. Dominique said her hoarding got much worse after her divorce, and she believes she was protecting herself from future romantic pain. Joan, the woman you met in Chapter 1, had experienced terrible abuse in her life, including sexual abuse, and she used stuff to wall herself off from intruders. A house full of things would certainly keep anyone, including men, from entering her life. There was literally no room for anyone else. My clients often mention that they find it soothing to be around their possessions. Having a lot of things—they say—may substitute for the emotional needs that are not being fulfilled through personal relationships, while at the same time, ironically, impeding these relationships from forming. Some people who don't have satisfaction in their personal relationships transfer the need to connect to their stuff, which they then feel overly connected to. I've seen this with people who hoard animals as well. They receive unconditional love and attention from their many pets, even when they have so many they can't care for them all properly.

Many people say they simply don't have time to keep their environment organized, or to go through their things and get rid of stuff. And people are very busy. But just as when someone says he cannot afford to buy something, what he really means is that he needs to or would rather spend his money on other things, when someone says she doesn't have time to get organized and get rid of things, she means that she'd prefer to or needs to use the time for other things.

And that's fine for some people, but I would argue that for most of us, failing to deal with your clutter, and avoiding devoting the time to making your environment a place of peace, is a losing proposition in the long run. It may seem easier at the time to not deal with your clutter, but overall, it makes life much harder and adds to your stress level.

Not everyone who has a cluttered living space has a cluttered psyche, of course, but it is true of some people, and is quite often true of those who compulsively hoard. I believe that there's a chicken-and-egg dynamic at play here: The mind is cluttered with too much and life is overwhelming, so disorganized thinking and a sense of distraction prevent you from keeping your living space organized; in turn, looking at a disorganized living space causes stress—that pile of papers is a reminder of one more chore you haven't gotten to, and adds to your

WHAT DOES YOUR STUFF SYMBOLIZE?

This is an exercise to help you determine what your stuff may mean to you. Simply ask yourself the questions that follow about items that you're not sure why you keep, or things that you have multiple versions of. Knowing why you save things can help you decide if you really want to keep them, or if they could be thrown out or given a more useful home with someone else.

1. What do you feel when you see the item? Does it make you feel good? Or does it bring up negative feelings, such as sadness or regret?

2. How did you acquire the item? Did it belong to someone else? The history of an item, whether it was a gift or whether it belonged to someone important to you, can play into your feelings about it.

3. Why do you think you keep it?

4. What do you think it would mean about you if you got rid of it? Would you feel wasteful, for instance, or like you were giving up something more than the material item, like a part of your history or identity?

5. What do you fear would happen if you let go of the item? Do you fear what others would think if they knew that you got rid of the item? Sometimes people have unconscious fears about what others would think if they got rid of something a friend or family member once gave them.

sense of being overwhelmed and distracted. It's a cycle that takes practice and behavioral change to reverse.

Just as someone who is depressed or doesn't think highly of himself might not put a lot of attention into how he looks, in the same way he may not put a lot of effort into keeping his environment neat and functional. What's more, I've heard people say time and again that they're often motivated to clean up for others, if someone is coming over, but not for themselves. "If someone came over, I'd make things look nice," says Anita—not by truly cleaning up and organizing, though, because she becomes overwhelmed at the prospect. "Things would be stashed everywhere to create that look," she laughs.

Why we keep what we keep has to do with the life we've lived, the kind of environment we were raised in, and in some cases the traumatic things that have happened to us in our past. For non-hoarders, it may be that there's nothing terribly symbolic about a particular item; it may simply be that you have trouble organizing, or you have distortions that are keeping you from making good decisions and having a more organized home. If you like something and you have a place for it, there's nothing wrong with keeping it.

But if you're feeling overwhelmed by a particular item or type of item (if your desk is piled high with papers, for instance, and you can't seem to find what you need and make a dent in the pile), it's worthwhile to think about why you're having a hard time letting go of or organizing your things. Being able to understand your motivation for keeping your possessions, as well as your reluctance to clean or organize them, will help you make the kinds of lasting changes that will create a less stressful life.

CHAPTER 3

"You Love Your Stuff More Than Me"

LIKE MANY PSYCHOLOGICAL CONDITIONS, compulsive hoarding is one for which many people don't generally seek help until they are forced to or after they have hit rock bottom. A sufferer will often live in a deep well of denial, stepping carefully over heaps of belongings, sometimes enduring health-threatening conditions in an environment that prevents others from getting close to her. It's hard to imagine what could feel worse than that, what could bring someone further into the depths of despair, so that she finally feels motivated to get help.

What "rock bottom" looks like to an individual is subjective and varies according to a person's circumstances. It could be that her home is at imminent risk of being condemned; the state or municipality is looking closely at removing children or pets from the home for their own safety; or, more often, her spouse or children are so frustrated and so scared for her safety that they deliver an ultimatum: It's us, or your stuff.

Mary Ann was faced with such an ultimatum from her family, who, in similar words, said they were at their own bottom. Married with two teenage children, Mary Ann was never a tidy person, and clutter in her home escalated to a Level 4 following her mom's death from cancer. Her mother had lived with the family, and one of the activities that she and her mother enjoyed doing together was going to

53

garage sales. Mary Ann continued to scour garage and yard sales after her mother passed. She was unable to get rid of anything that had belonged to her mother, and began to fill the room her mother had once inhabited with various treasures she found on her solo excursions.

The interesting thing was that she wasn't bringing home items she would have normally purchased; she was purchasing things that she believed her mom would like. She felt somehow that having them would make her mother happy, even though her mom was no longer living.

Once her mother's old room was full, the "treasures" began to take over the living room, then dining room, and finally started spreading into the kids' rooms. Everywhere you looked there were books, dolls, stuffed animals, clothing, and ceramics. Repeated protests from her kids did not motivate her to change. And at first, Mary Ann's husband, Tim, encouraged the kids to be patient because he felt that she needed to grieve the loss of her mother.

Eventually, though, the problem grew to the point where the children's closets were so full they had difficulty accessing their clothing. It had been months since the children had friends over. Not only were they embarrassed about their environment, but there was no place to play. The family was having financial trouble because of Mary Ann's shopping. The kids had to shop for their clothes at secondhand stores. They were living from paycheck to paycheck; Mary Ann had spent the family's savings.

After 9 months, Tim finally felt that he was in a position to set limits, for his, his family's, and Mary Ann's well-being. She was so far into her acquiring behaviors that she didn't know how to get out. I see this frequently. When the person starts feeling too much shame, guilt, and embarrassment, it becomes even harder to reach out.

In an "I've had it" moment, Tim called the kids together, and the three of them approached Mary Ann with their concerns and offered an ultimatum. Tim told her that he would move the kids to his parents' home that night unless she agreed to seek help, and he would not sleep at home either. In tears and pleading with her family, Mary Ann promised them she would get things under control, to just give her a chance. Tim refused, saying she had to consult a specialist, which was when I was called. Now, keep in mind, threats and ultimatums are not the place to start. But when a person's hoarding behaviors get to the point where the family is at risk, and they see no other alternative, sometimes this approach is necessary.

Mary Ann's family's intervention did motivate her to get the help she needed, and her story had a happy ending: Mary Ann was able to work through her grief, and address her hoarding behavior. The family was eventually able to live in a relatively neat, organized home once again. But often the way a family tries to help is positively heartbreaking. Dina, 41, recalls her family's interaction with her beloved aunt, who battled compulsive hoarding and obesity. "So many people judged her about her hoarding, in addition to her weight, but no one considered her contributions to the community," recalls Dina, who said her aunt was well known in the neighborhood for her outgoing nature and willingness to volunteer her time at various local organizations. (Dina believed her aunt had gained weight in part because she couldn't move around her home.)

"The family badgered, belittled, and shamed her for her problem," says Dina. "It was as if they were mad at her for it, rather than trying to understand it, which was so frustrating to me. I'd bring up how the family treated her, and she'd always just say, 'Oh, sweetheart, don't worry about it.'" Dina used to leave the room when her mother and other relatives spoke ill of her aunt, and her nonverbal disapproval silently influenced them to speak more gently in front of Dina. Still, Dina couldn't get them to see that they weren't helping to solve the problem by getting angry and judging and attacking her aunt.

Ultimately, Dina's aunt died of a heart attack, and there was some question about whether she would have survived if the paramedics had been able to lay her down flat to administer CPR. "It wasn't until after she died that my mother realized all that she did for the community, because of everyone who spoke out at her funeral. I could tell that then she felt sorry for how she treated her," recalls Dina. Unfortunately, there was no making it up to her.

A WHOLE FAMILY PROBLEM

If you're not a person with a hoarding problem, it is understandable that you might find it truly baffling and infuriating when your needs and concerns aren't considered by a loved one who hoards. It's hard to watch someone seem to "choose" piles of what most people would consider to be garbage over you.

I believe strongly in treating the whole family of a person who hoards, because there are so many complex dynamics, resentments, and unresolved issues that feed into the sufferer's behavior. I try to remind family members that while I understand why it seems like the sufferer is "choosing" his stuff over the family, it's not a straightforward choice. Compulsive hoarding is an illness, not a preference. No one goes to high school thinking he can't wait until he graduates so he can fulfill his dreams of hoarding. It is a condition, like alcoholism or depression, that leads people to behave in ways they wouldn't otherwise and make choices that someone who is not impaired by the faulty reasoning of the condition wouldn't make. Expecting someone with hoarding to simply wake up one day and stop acquiring and clean up their house is like expecting an alcoholic to wake up one day and stop drinking. (Compulsive hoarding is not considered to be an addiction per se, but the condition does involve compulsions, as do addictions; sufferers do take pleasure in acquiring and find it extremely difficult to stop, despite the negative consequences.) Even though we think of cleaning up after ourselves as a normal and natural part of life, for some people it truly is not, and it can be extremely difficult to learn even if the person wants to.

Of course, you don't have to live with a hoarder to experience the strain that clutter can place on a relationship. Perhaps you feel you've been hounded by your spouse for months to clean out the garage, or have felt the frustration of not being able to find what you need due to a chaotic, cluttered living space. Sometimes relationships are also negatively affected because people living together in a home have different tolerance levels for chaos in general. Many people with multiple pets wrestle with this kind of conflict. David, who lives with his wife and two sons, was frustrated by his wife's pet bird and the fact that he felt the bird was and had always been her priority, even early on in their relationship. After they'd been together a couple of years, David took a job in another state, and his wife got a parrot to keep her company. In his absence, she let the parrot have the run of their apartment. When he came back, he found the home in disrepair. "The bird would chew the covers of books, and it was disgusting— there was bird poop everywhere," he recalls. "I don't think she would say that the bird was her priority, but she also didn't want to give up the bird even though she knew I was unhappy about it."

David repeatedly complained about the bird's mess, and expressed that he wanted to have more control over his environment. His wife listened to his concerns and understood his point of view, but in David's opinion, she overidentified with the bird and worried it would be sad to have its freedom curtailed if she put it in a cage. "When we would talk about the bird, she wanted to make me happy and felt bad that these things bothered me, but she also couldn't set any limits for the bird. The only thing I could do was end the relationship, and I didn't want to do that. There are always things you have to live with that you don't like, and I figured that bird was one of them." Fortunately, David and his wife went to couples therapy and worked out a compromise: The bird would have her wings clipped, and eventually they moved into a larger house where the bird could have limited freedom. Because they were both willing to compromise, things worked out, but I know many situations in which the ending is not so happy.

EVERYDAY CONFLICTS OVER CLUTTER

Even in non-hoarded homes, arguments over whose turn it is to do the three days' worth of dirty dishes that have piled up, or to organize the gigantic baskets of hats and mittens and scarves that have been thrown in with random rain boots and other belongings, aren't always about the stuff itself. The mess is a trigger topic that leads to the airing of other, often deeper grievances between family members. I have watched conversations about clutter escalate very quickly, when blame begins to surface, accusations fly, and defensiveness blocks any form of effective communication or resolution.

I have also known non-hoarders who nonetheless feel the need to hide purchases from their spouses to avoid their disapproval. Such secrecy or conflict can take its toll on a partnership. "My husband thinks I have too many clothes, and I'd rather not get into it with him, so I stick my bags in my closet and unpack them later, when he's not around," admits Judy, a working mom of one who is not struggling with hoarding issues. Judy agrees that she has lots of clothes, but feels that she earns money and is entitled to buy herself things if she likes, and feels her husband is judgmental and controlling about her shopping habits.

Whether or not she has "too many" clothes is beside the point here; at issue is the stress she experiences in sneaking around with her purchases and not addressing her grievances with her husband directly. In their case, I believe that issues around stuff are an expression of other issues in their relationship, and probably not the main problem between them.

While non-hoarders do not typically put their loved ones in danger by creating fire hazards or unsanitary conditions, living with someone whose mind is cluttered in part because their life is cluttered can be exasperating. One woman I know says that her kids get upset when she doesn't remember to sign their permission slips for class trips. Once she takes the forms out of their backpacks, she often forgets where she put them. She even sent them off to school on a day when the school was closed, because her e-mail inbox is so full that she missed

DOES YOUR CLUTTER CAUSE CONFLICT?

One person can look at a room and see it as a little disorganized, whereas his spouse can view it as living in chaos. Below are some things to think about if you are the messy one in the house.

☐ Do you and your family argue or have passive tension over your mess?

☐ Do you feel that your family would like you to be neater or more organized even if they don't say so?

☐ Even if you value your family's comfort and happiness in the home, do your actions or inactions convey otherwise?

☐ Does your personal stuff often spread into other areas of the house?

☐ Do you have trouble finding things because there is no organizational system, and do the consequences of this (lateness, for instance) negatively impact your family members?

☐ Do your kids or spouse hesitate to have people over because of the state of the house?

☐ Are family members unable to use certain areas of the home because of your stuff?

If you answered yes to even one of these questions, you and your family are experiencing unnecessary stress due to the clutter in your environment. If you answered yes to more than one, your relationship to your things may well be interfering with your relationships with the people you live with. A proactive stance—calling your family together to let them know that you're aware of the problem and that you're going to begin to chip away at it—will go a long way in improving your relationships. You may even want to ask for your family's support in helping you get a handle on your clutter.

the e-mails from the school administrators. A cluttered mind can interfere with your ability to be present and mindful with your family.

IF YOU LIVE WITH SOMEONE
WHO HOARDS

Even though compulsive hoarding is a psychological condition and not
willful behavior, the children and spouses of those who hoard can't be
expected to have endless patience. This isn't necessarily a bad thing,
because quite often it's the family's push to set boundaries that makes
the difference in getting someone help. But there's a fine line between
putting constructive pressure on a person who hoards to face her issues,
and expressing negative feelings that will only drive the person further
into isolation and cause greater rifts within the family.

By the same token, there's another fine line between being patient
and nonjudgmental toward a person who hoards (both of which are
absolutely necessary if you want to help the person) and being so
patient that you enable and adapt to their way of living and don't vocal-
ize your own needs. In fact, many people who live with hoarders simply give in to the situation—they don't even see the point in cleaning up
after themselves after a while. The hoarder's mess is going to engulf
them in any case, so why bother?

If you live with someone who hoards or who has a problem with
keeping clutter under control, it's important to bear in mind that the
mess is only the symptom of a deeper psychological issue. The individual might have attention problems that manifest themselves in an
inability to finish a project, or he might struggle with procrastination
and perfectionism. These are not things that are easily overcome, no
matter how frustrating they are to the people you love. Anita, the
25-year-old woman who likes to hold on to clothing from various stages
of her life, admits that she has a very messy room, and she wants to

THE 10 LEAST HELPFUL THINGS YOU CAN SAY TO A CLUTTERER

If you live with someone who is messy or keeps common areas cluttered, chances are you have the same arguments weekly—or even daily. While it's important to express your needs, it's also important to facilitate open communication and to keep tempers under control so that you can work toward actually solving the problem. Here's a list of statements that you should look to avoid; each of these will simply cause the person to feel judged, and will decrease the likelihood of sustainable, positive change.

1. "You don't care about yourself or your environment."

2. "You don't care about how your clutter affects me."

3. "You must have a disorganized mind."

4. "It's not important for you to have things organized."

5. "You're a slob!"

6. "Your stuff is more important than me!"

7. "Just throw it away! It's no big deal!"

8. "You don't need to keep that."

9. "You're never going to use/wear that."

10. "Just get rid of it. You won't miss it."

make it better. "I sometimes think I can't take it anymore and have to come up with a system," she says. Yet whenever she begins organizing her things, she has a hard time focusing. (Right now she tosses stuff on top of her dresser or in bins under her bed and doesn't know where the items she needs are located.) "Any organizing project that I have to do feels like work for me, not fun. I just want my mind to be free and to let it go where it wants. I'm constantly moving things around in my room and redecorating, but it's not really solving the problem."

THE 10 MOST HELPFUL THINGS TO SAY TO A CLUTTERER

Below is a list of the most helpful things you can say to facilitate a positive dialogue with the clutterer in your life. It might help to make a copy of this list and place it in a visible area, so when conflicts around clutter arise, you can use this script to better communicate.

1. "I know this is hard for you."

2. "Let me know how I can help."

3. "You don't have to fix this problem overnight."

4. "Let's find ways to simplify the process."

5. "Don't look at the big picture. Take baby steps."

6. "When you get overwhelmed, take a break and remember your goal is to live a healthier life."

7. "We are a team!"

8. "Help me understand where you have the most difficulty."

9. "What things are important to you in your home?"

10. "Let me know how I can best support you; you are in charge of how this process of decluttering goes."

Anita lives with roommates and keeps her chaos confined to her room, but conflict in a cluttered home is almost inevitable. Sarah, 37, a mom of a 10-year-old, shares a home with a man who was never required to clean up after himself, and she feels frustrated with him quite often. There's always a pile of his stuff on the floor, and his dirty plates fill the sink. His clothes are tossed all over their bedroom, and unless she picks them up, there they stay. "I knew that he didn't clean up after himself when I married him, so I can't expect him to change his ways," Sarah says. "I have to learn to live with the clutter, but psychologically I feel defeated and resentful because I'm constantly cleaning up after him."

And when she's feeling hungry, angry, lonely, or tired (HALT), the stress is worse. Sarah has considered a housekeeper, but believes that unless the housekeeper lived with them, which they can't afford, there would be 6 days of buildup for 1 day of clean. A housekeeper also would do nothing to resolve the problem and would simply enable it. "Our marriage works in other ways, because we are so aligned in our values," she says, but Sarah dislikes feeling that she has to act like his mother by cleaning up after him. The stress and emotional clutter between them puts a strain on their relationship. Living with a clutterer can make you feel as though your time and space aren't being considered or respected, especially if you are constantly cleaning up to make the environment more habitable. And, as the problem continues, resentment can build, further exacerbating the conflict already present in the relationship.

FAMILIARITY BREEDS CONTEMPT

When I was working with Mary Ann in her home, her daughter mentioned that when I pointed out a problem to her mother, Mary Ann was willing to listen, but when her daughter said the exact same thing, she'd react defensively.

While it might seem logical that someone would value the opinions of the people they love and cherish over those of a stranger, a certain amount of familiarity can breed contempt when it comes to this kind of constructive criticism. Perhaps the person who has difficulty with clutter feels that his family member has ulterior motives, like wanting to control him, or that the family member is not perfect either and so has no right to criticize. Family relationships are very complex, with histories and repeated patterns of behavior that can complicate what appear to be simple issues on the surface. In the case of a professional like myself, the relationship is more businesslike and so less emotionally complicated. Unlike a family member, who has a stake in the situation (she wants to live in a cleaner environment), an outsider provides objective distance on the situation. Of course I care deeply about my clients' welfare, and do everything I can to help motivate them to begin living cleaner, happier, clutter-free lives. But at the end of the day, I can go home.

When the problem is more serious than clutter—if the person is actually hoarding—it often pays to have a therapist, or at least a neutral party that the person who hoards accepts is there to help, once the process of clearing out begins. Ideally, the family is there for support and an extra push, and in some cases, a friend who can be encouraging can also help. My goal when I treat people who hoard is to teach everyone involved how to help the person who hoards think differently about his stuff and help him through the decision making that will eventually lead to an organized home. Working with an entire family involves helping everyone, not just the person who hoards, think differently about the problem, so they can be supportive and not allow frustrations to get in the way of progress.

An outsider can also be helpful when the problem is persistent cluttering, although the role of the outsider is somewhat different. You don't want to insert a friend between you and your loved one in a conflict, but if you're the person who clutters, it can be tremendously helpful to have the objectivity of a friend when you're cleaning, purging, or organizing. That person is not sentimentally attached to your possessions and can help you make better decisions about what to keep and what to get rid of. There's also an emotional benefit to just having a friend around while you're doing an unpleasant task such as cleaning out your closet. Having someone else with you also helps to make you accountable—if you make a date to declutter your basement at 2:00 p.m. on Saturday, and you know your friend is showing up, you're less likely to put it off.

Some of the tougher family dynamics I encounter occur when a client's hoarding behavior seems to be a direct reaction to the relational problems within the family itself. The hoarding may be a form of rebellion against a family member—"This is my space, you can't control me!"—or a certain type of dependency, a tacit request for others to take care of him. In David's situation with the bird, he and his wife half-joked that the bird was "punishment" for the fact that he'd left for a year. As mentioned earlier, hoarding can also be a sign that an individual is not happy in their life or other relationships. This is also a fairly common theme with people who clutter.

A few years ago, I treated a woman named Candice, who had a young daughter with very mild cerebral palsy. Her relationship with her husband was distant, and the clutter was a way of distracting herself from the depressing feeling inside their home. Her husband was always gone when I came to the house to work with her, and would not come to any sessions at the clinic. He complained constantly about Candice's mess, but did nothing to help keep the house in order. He felt as though it was not his responsibility.

But while Candice did have the primary hoarding problem, her husband contributed to the mess, leaving used dishes in the sink, whiskers on the bathroom counter, and laundry in the basket. And because Candice felt guilty about her daughter's condition and felt her daughter had enough to manage, she never encouraged her to clean up either. Mind you, Candice's daughter was in elementary school, earned good grades, and was social with other kids. There was no reason to think that a few household chores would be too much for her to handle. I believe that since Candice was overwhelmed herself, she projected those feelings onto her daughter, and assumed that she felt the same way.

Candice was treated in my Intensive Outpatient Program, which is comprised of 6 weeks of 4-hour sessions, 5 days per week, with 1 to 2 hours of homework each night. The first 2 weeks consisted of education, training, and therapy in which Candice addressed the reasons she had difficulty letting go of things. We also practiced purging with paperwork she brought in from her home.

On week 3 we began to work directly in her home. When we worked together, she did well, but she struggled with keeping it up on her own and completing the homework when I wasn't around. She had no support from her husband and struggled with making sure her daughter did her chores; she was conflicted about it to begin with. Candice found treatment frustrating.

In situations like Candice's, where someone doesn't have the benefit of a supportive family, I try to help the person do as much as she can for herself. Much of Candice's therapy revolved around identifying her needs, encouraging her to set firm boundaries with her husband, and focusing on what she felt she could do on her own to improve her situation. In an ideal world, everyone would be on board, but we all have to do the best we can with what we have.

As is the experience for many people who are trying to overcome a deep-seated problem, follow-through after therapy can be much more difficult than you might think. Imagine an alcoholic in a month-long treatment program; they're accountable on a daily basis to a counselor and peers. When the program ends, that person has to stick with new learning and a new lifestyle without daily support. That can be incredibly challenging (and that's why peer-support groups can be so helpful). Outside of therapy, old hoarding patterns can sneak back quickly, and with them, the old, maladaptive reasons to keep things and procrastinate on making decisions. That's exactly what happened with Candice.

I also think that part of her difficulty with follow-through came from feeling discouraged with her life overall. Candice is a classic story of how unhappiness in relationships causes depression, frustration, lack of attention, distraction, and a certain degree of resignation.

While Candice's husband refused to help, he did let Candice know where he stood. Sometimes the dynamic around clutter can be more subtle, a passive-aggressive way of communicating between spouses. Judy believes that her husband semi-deliberately leaves his coffee grounds and filter system in the sink when he makes his coffee because he knows it bothers her. "I usually just put it in the dishwasher, but it makes me angry and I think he gets a little bit of a victory out of it," she says. On the few occasions she's spoken up about how she feels, his response is that he was going to get to it eventually. Still, he might then take several hours to do so, during which she feels compelled to ask him again—and then she feels like a nag. "The conflict isn't worth it, so I just do it myself," she says.

The place to start for any family member or friend of someone who hoards is to set aside judgment. That is not easy to do. Compulsive hoarding is such a visible problem and one that affects each family member personally. But we all have things we fear being judged upon. What's more, remembering that compulsive hoarding is not a choice is critical, as is remembering that this problem is only part of the person you care about. The person who hoards or clutters is not just "a hoarder" or "a clutterer." She may also be a good friend, a terrific baker, a loving grandmother, and countless other things.

The second thing to do is to educate yourself about the condition of hoarding, as you are doing now, which will go a long way in helping you to better understand the complexities of this condition. Understanding those who hoard, and how the behaviors and resulting chaotic environment can create intense feelings of shame, guilt, and embarrassment, can help you approach the person with compassion and patience, and convey how you feel without anger.

The third thing is to anticipate that helping someone overcome her clutter problem, no matter where she is on the continuum, will likely be frustrating for both of you at times. The forthcoming chapters will outline ways that someone who struggles with cluttering can improve her situation. You can't fix the problem for another person, no matter how badly you want to, and in fact it is so important that the person with the hoarding or cluttering issues learns that she can work through it herself. Your role is one of supporter and cheerleader.

She must be in charge of her own process, or any improvements in the home will not last.

Finally, be prepared to compromise. Your goal, if you're helping someone who hoards or anyone who clutters, is to find that middle ground where you can both be comfortable. Andrea, whose daughter Lisa had been begging her to get help for years, for instance, felt like Lisa was trying to control her when she made suggestions as to what might be thrown out. As a neutral party, I was able to suggest to Andrea that this wasn't the case. "What motivation would your daughter have in wanting to control you?" I asked her. Andrea was able to see, at least in the moment, that her daughter had no ulterior motives but to strengthen their relationship and to help her mother live more safely. For Lisa's part, I encouraged her not to try to fix her mother, but rather work toward making the home more livable.

One of the many ironies of this condition is that the person who hoards feels like she would be giving up control if she allowed others to make decisions about her stuff. By keeping herself surrounded by stuff, she believes she's retaining control. But her environment is so out of control that her sense of control is simply an illusion. It's like someone with OCD who washes his hands over and over again to feel a sense of control over an impending disease, but who is clearly controlled by the behavior.

One of the reasons I work with all family members when treating hoarders is that there are often codependency issues involved. Code-pendent relationships typically develop out of good intentions. Recall Amanda, the woman who lived with her parents and spent her days shopping online. In talking with her parents about Amanda's hoarding, it was clear that some of their personal struggles as children were influencing their inability to set boundaries with their daughter. For example, Amanda's father reported that he grew up in an extremely rigid environment and swore that he would not impose that on his own children. Amanda's mother felt that growing up in a household where both parents were doctors and expected her to become a doctor had placed unusually high expectations on her—she, too, swore she would never do the same with her children. In trying to avoid the pressures they'd experienced growing up, they failed to place any expectations on Amanda, which contributed to Amanda's spending and hoarding behaviors.

In Amanda's parents' case, there were things they might have done to help her make positive changes. They might have limited the funds they gave her, or asked that while she lived at home, she be employed to contribute to the household, which might have given her an outlet aside from shopping and brought her out of herself. (Ultimately, they did do some of these things.) In case these strategies seem obvious when you read them, it must be noted that things are not always as clear to the person going through the problem. Most of us think we know what we would do in a given situation, but how do we really know until it happens to us? It's easier to judge, sometimes, than to try to understand.

WHEN THINGS CHANGE

Sometimes the loved one of someone who hoards may limit his intervention because he is, on some level, scared of failing and so seeing his worst fear realized: that the person hoarding really does value stuff more than human relationships. That dynamic may also have been at play with Tim and Mary Ann at first—what if she couldn't face her problem and he'd have to make good on his threat to move the kids out of the house? Things eventually escalated to the point where that prospect was less scary than the thought of continuing to live the way they'd been living.

I remember many years ago, before I was married, I was dating someone who had developed a drinking problem. I was at a point of despair, because I cared for him, but couldn't live with his drinking. He and I went to therapy together, and at the second session the therapist asked him point-blank, "Are you willing to give up alcohol to be with Robin?" He said no! Well, that really put me in my place. I was not more important to this man than alcohol. There it was, right out of his mouth.

It was hard to hear the truth at the time, but now I see that moment as a gift—my life would have been disastrous had I stayed with him. I believe that some spouses or children of people who hoard avoid confronting their loved one because the unknown is frightening: They would rather continue to live in an environment they don't like than risk changing their relationship with their loved one in a negative way.

When a relationship with someone who hoards does change, either because the person learns to manage her hoarding or because the spouse or child decides he or she is not going to tolerate it anymore, it can be terrifying for all involved. While it seems as if the hoarder is the sole source of the problems, the spouses and cohabitants also play a role, usually a passive or adaptive role. Familiar roles, even if they're not working, can become psychologically very comfortable for people.

While it is tempting just to work around the hoard and not assert one's space because it feels too overwhelming, making clear boundaries and insisting that the person who hoards (or clutters) respects those boundaries is crucial to the emotional health of the whole family. For instance, I encourage the spouse of someone who hoards to say, "This is my side of the bed, and I'm going to ask you not to put things on my side of the bed—it's important to me to get a good night's sleep." And if he does begin to clutter the bed, I encourage her to hand the item(s) back to him and ask him to put it elsewhere.

By asking the person who is cluttering to respect your space, you are modeling good habits, and thus keeping your own resentment in

TALKING TO A CLUTTERER

If you live with a person who clutters and you've been quietly (or not so quietly) struggling with how to speak to him or her about how the mess affects you, try this three-step process.

1. Bring up what you've noticed about the way clutter impacts all of your lives. Try to do so in a non-accusatory way, even if you're angry. You might try something like, "I've noticed that Dad gets really annoyed because he has to clear off the dining room table before we sit down," or "I've noticed that you've been late a lot because you haven't been able to find the car keys." Ask open-ended questions, rather than make accusations, and come from a place of concern, not anger. If you're too angry to talk about it, wait until you've calmed down before initiating the conversation.

2. Talk about how the mess affects you. When you limit your complaints to things that affect you directly, not only is the clutterer less likely to feel attacked, but it's very hard to argue with someone who is simply stating how they feel. "I feel upset when I have to move your books off the couch when I want to sit down. Could you please be more mindful of putting them away?" or "I know you care about how I feel, but when I tell you the cat's mess is upsetting to me and you don't clean it up, I feel like my feelings aren't important." You might have to be a broken record if the clutterer has tremendous difficulty changing her patterns, and many do. With time and practice, things can improve.

3. Get a neutral third party. Sometimes people who clutter can hear suggestions from a therapist, a life coach, or even a friend or non-immediate family member that they can't hear from you directly. Even if you think, "I've told her how I feel and she doesn't listen," a third-party assist can be helpful.

check by speaking up. Look for areas of agreement—"I'd like to ask if we can keep this part of the countertop clutter-free so I can make a sandwich"—and maintain that boundary. This will not "cure" someone who tends toward messiness and disorganization, but it will help keep your relationship from getting engulfed in the mess as well.

I'm often asked on my Facebook page if people ever just say to heck with it and give up on the person who hoards. Sadly, yes, that happens, although usually only after years of effort on the part of the family member to get through to the person. The bottom line with any psychological problem or bad habit is that we can't fix anybody else. People have to want to change, and no amount of trying is going to help if the person doesn't want to. A codependency trap that many children and loved ones of hoarding sufferers fall into is thinking or hoping that they will be the one to change the person, to fix the problem, and they get a sense of identity and purpose from that role. Unfortunately, unless the person who hoards wants to change, that situation ends in disappointment.

Quite often, though, persistent effort on the part of the loved one, as well as reasonable expectations (not "fixing" the person, but helping him get his environment to a place where you can have a good relationship with him and visit), can really help. No matter the outcome, I do encourage the loved ones of hoarding sufferers to take care of themselves, though, and that sometimes means detaching. You may be too invested in helping your loved one if you're not able to focus on your own life and relationships, or if you're getting depressed and angry about the situation. That's when it's time to say, "This isn't healthy for me anymore. I love you and you're important to me, but I focused more on getting you well than on my own life, and I can't do that anymore."

By now, you have a sense of how complex our relationships with our things can be, and how far our cluttering behaviors can extend, in our own lives and those of our loved ones. While overcoming compulsive hoarding is difficult, every one of us, no matter where on the continuum we fall, can improve our habits and consequently reduce our level of emotional clutter. That takes patience and compassion, and the tools you'll read about in upcoming chapters.

CHAPTER 4

PLACING YOURSELF ON THE CONTINUUM

THROUGHOUT THIS BOOK, I've made a distinction between people who hoard compulsively, whose hoarding significantly impairs their functioning, and non-hoarders.

But among clutterers, just as among hoarders, there are degrees. Read through the profiles starting below and think about which one you most identify with. You might find you identify with more than one, which is fine.

1. CLEAR AND CLEAN

Your Home: You cannot stand clutter, and your home looks perfectly orderly, with very few personal effects visible and those that are on display neatly arrayed. There are no dishes in the sink; all surfaces are clear; the beds are made; and clothing, toys, and reading materials are put away. What little is out on the desk is contained in neat piles or folders, and the TV remotes are all in one place, likely next to the TV. Closets and drawers are kept neat and organized, as is the kitchen pantry.

Your Habits: You tend to think long and hard about any purchase or item before bringing it home. You dispose of or put things away

73

as soon as you think of it, and ask yourself why you should keep something, rather than why you should throw it away. You find it a soothing form of stress relief to organize your things, and you might feel irritated when you see stuff that has no proper home. If you have pets, they are well groomed and cared for.

2. NEAT BUT DYNAMIC

Your Home: There's a place for most everything, and odds are the coats are hung on their hooks and the shoes are in the shoe area by the door, but on any given day, you might find an item ordered off the Internet that needs to be returned sitting in the entryway, and a pile of mail unopened on the kitchen counter, along with a dish or two that didn't quite make it to the sink. The coffee table and den areas are clean, but there is a half-done jigsaw puzzle sitting on the floor, and two or three books or periodicals on the end table, and a DVD still in the player, with the case nearby. Your clothes are hung up or put away and are easy to find, if not exactly neat. Your bathroom is clean, but you have more products and things around than you use every day.

　　Your Habits: You like a functional house, but tidiness isn't mandatory at all times. You leave projects or chores for a few hours or even a day or two, but you will get to them. You are pretty organized, and you can get rid of things without much difficulty if you no longer need them. You like to relax in a low-stress environment when you get home.

3. CONTROLLED CHAOS

Your Home: Your house has "areas" for things—a coat area, a toy area—rather than a place for every item. There's a lot of stuff visible, such as piles of children's artwork, a bookshelf with double rows of books and photo albums piled on top, and a crafts table with bins of supplies and stacks of half-done projects. There are boxes of photos and other items that you need to sort through at some point. Your clothes are mostly put away, but not necessarily neatly, and there may well be several days' worth of outfits draped on chairs. Your kitchen is not dirty, but there are sometimes dishes in the sink for a day or two, and you've seen an occasional ant. Even when your home has just been cleaned, there is still a sense of a lot of stuff. If you have pets, they are well cared for, but there might be pet hair on furniture, and occasionally you can smell them. Even when your house is neat, there's a killer closet somewhere that if opened could cause a small avalanche.

Your Habits: There's a lot of life in this house, and you would rather spend your time doing things—projects, cooking, reading, or other activities—than cleaning and organizing. Not enough time is taken between activities to properly put things away before the next project is started, and not every possession has a distinct home. There are organizing systems—bins, usually—but things are not generally returned to the right bin, and there is not a regular schedule of sorting through things. You procrastinate on going through items and making decisions, although you're not particularly sentimentally attached to your stuff—you simply think you might need it. Every so often you get frustrated with the state of your home and go on a cleaning and organizing spree.

4. CLUTTER CRISIS

Your Home: No one would call you someone who hoards—you can walk through the hallways, and you can sit on the sofa without having to remove items—but there is stuff all over the place: piles of unread magazines by the easy chair, evidence of dinner having been eaten at the coffee table (because the dining room table is covered in piles of paperwork), shoes strewn around various rooms, coats draped over the back of the couch. Your kitchen is a bit out of control—your refrigerator is stuffed with food (some of which should probably be thrown away), and you've been known to resort to paper plates because you've run out of clean dishes. The bathroom could use a good cleaning, and your bedroom has piles of clothing on the bed and floor because there's not enough room in your closets to store what you own. If you live with others, you have heard about how your clutter impacts them negatively.

Your Habits: You feel like you are just too busy and tired when you get home to deal with your house, and so you treat it a bit like a hotel—in, sleep, and out. You'd like it to be cleaner and better organized—you don't have one place where you put your keys every day, for instance—but the thought of dealing with it on the weekends is just too unappealing, so you clean what's important (the kitchen and bathroom) but never get around to putting much away, except perhaps when you're having company. You also have lots of stuff—you like to shop, perhaps, but you don't give much thought to what you should get rid of when you bring new purchases into your house. You often can't find things you need, which causes you stress. Every so often, you'll power organize one area, and then lose interest in the rest of the house.

5. BORDERLINE HOARDING

Your Home: Things are getting out of hand. If you have a pet, you can tell immediately because the litter box needs to be changed or there's hair covering the furniture. You may have a problem with ants or roaches in your kitchen because dishes sit around too long and food isn't properly sealed. You have rooms in your house that you don't really use because they've become storage areas for projects, equipment, and just plain "stuff." Your desk is piled high with papers and receipts, and the corners of your room and the bottom of the staircase contain piles or shopping bags full of things that you've been meaning to get to, like hand-me-downs to pass along or other things to donate. You're not swimming in stuff—your hallways are passable—and there's no physical danger, but things are quite chaotic, and it's not uncommon that you might step on some papers or kick a box aside in an attempt to get where you're going.

Your Habits: You have close friends over, but if there's a book group meeting, you try not to have it at your house because you're a little embarrassed and feel you don't have the time or energy to clean up. You have no good systems for organization, and what's more, you have a lot of stuff, and your valuable things are on the shelf right next to less valuable items. You don't go through your things and get rid of unused items, preferring to just move them up to the attic or down to the basement, where they sit and sometimes get ruined from the dust and possibly even mildew. You love your pets, but sometimes you don't take the time to clean up after them. The messier the house gets, the less you feel like dealing with it, so you don't.

As you can see, there are degrees of clutter, and much of what is tolerable for a person depends on how much stress the clutter causes her and her family. And of course, if more than one member of a household has cluttering tendencies, things can quickly get out of hand.

Number 5, the Borderline Hoarding, begins to head into the mild range of compulsive hoarding, depending on the degree to which the individual's belongings get in the way of the rest of his life, how much strife it causes at home, and how anxious that person feels when asked to get rid of things. The more intense any of these factors are for an individual, the further along the continuum he is.

There are many ways clutter can impact our quality of life, even if it's not at the level at which someone would be thought to suffer from compulsive hoarding issues. Naturally, the further along on the

THE 10 WAYS CLUTTER CAN CAUSE YOU STRESS

1. It's hard to locate the things you need, when you need them.

2. Being unable to locate important papers, like bills, birth certificates, tax documents, passports, or driver's licenses, can result in major setbacks and financial penalties.

3. Arguments over mess can strain your relationships with family members. And difficulty finding the things you need can cause your family members to be late for their appointments, which leads to more stress.

4. You spend money on things you already own, because you have forgotten you have them or can't find them.

5. Looking at a pile of bills or any mess is a constant reminder of a chore that needs to be done.

6. A cluttered bedroom is difficult to relax in, and can affect the quality of your sleep and your intimate life.

7. Keeping too many reminders from your past can distract you from living in the present.

8. A cluttered room can overstimulate your senses and cause you to feel anxious or unable to relax.

9. Having to move things around to use your space effectively (i.e., to sit at the kitchen table or sleep in your bed) wastes time and creates extra work.

10. Reluctance to invite people into your home because it's not neat can lead to social isolation, which extensive research suggests can negatively impact your health.

continuum you are, the more stressful life can get. Cassie, a 51-year-old wife and mother, is at the Clutter Crisis level. Her home is quite messy, and some rooms are worse than others. "I have a lot of papers and magazines and newspapers, and I want to recycle them, and not just throw them in the trash," she explains. "I also have lots of jars, gift bags, and silk flowers that came on presents. Can't they be reused? I have a hard time deciding what to throw out, and I just don't want to deal with it."

Consequently, Cassie, who is job hunting, cannot find her references, although she thinks they're somewhere in her desk. Her husband also has some issues with clutter—he sees value in many things and prevents Cassie from getting rid of certain items because he thinks he might need them. So between the two of them, their house is quite disorganized. There is tension between them because of the clutter, and Cassie feels like a failure when she looks around and sees the mess. She tends to move things to the basement rather than make decisions about them, which clinicians refer to a term called churning—the mess is moved from place to place, but never truly dealt with.

When I suggest that it would be easier to organize than to deal with her constant anxiety about the mess, she agrees, but says she has other things she would rather do when she gets home, and has a hard time seeing unpleasant projects through to the end. She also notes that her husband's mother used to throw away his things without his permission, once getting rid of his prized model train set while he was at school. Cassie says this continued even into adulthood; when they went on their honeymoon, his mother cleaned out his old bedroom and had turned it into a game room by the time they got back. It's easy to understand why he feels protective of his belongings and why she is extra careful not to throw anything of his away without his permission, but that knowledge doesn't make their home any less frustrating for both of them to live in.

How Much Is Too Much?

I've often heard people half-joke that they don't have too much stuff, but that their apartments or closets are simply too small to accommodate the perfectly reasonable amount of stuff that they have. And in the case of people with tiny apartments and a great love of collecting, that may well be the case. Certainly, if you put Imelda Marcos's shoe collection into a typical New York City studio apartment, it would look like a hoarded home, with floor-to-ceiling footwear. This demonstrates that the concept of "too much" stuff depends on several factors in addition to the sheer volume of your belongings.

These factors are highly individual and depend on who you are, what you need, your space restrictions, how passionately you feel about your possessions, your tolerance for disorganization, the opinions of those you live with, and many other criteria. One man's "collection" is another's pile of junk; one woman's good deal is her husband's idea of a colossal waste of money. For that reason, I think it's useful to tease out the differences between a reasonable situation and one that is perhaps on its way to becoming out of hand, if it isn't already. It will also help you figure out where you are on the clutter continuum, and where your weakness lies—in acquisition, disorganization, or difficulty getting rid of things.

COLLECTING VERSUS STOCKPILING

Webster's dictionary defines a collection as "an accumulation of objects gathered for study, comparison, or exhibition or as a hobby." Fair enough, but sometimes collections can take over your home. A collector is someone who has an interest in a specific area or type of item, and he will typically research and plan how to add to his collection, and perhaps have a plan for the entire collection (to eventually donate it to a historical society, for instance, or to pass it on to his grandkids).

But some people confuse collecting with accumulating or even stockpiling. One woman I worked with had a large "collection" of animal figurines she'd ordered from the Home Shopping Network and various Web sites because they were "such a good deal," and having lots of animals around appealed to her. They were not particularly sought-after or unique or rare figurines, nor were they especially valuable. She simply thought they were pretty and couldn't resist buying them, and now they were cluttering up her entire house. For her, they represented companionship. She named every one of them and attached personal stories to them.

These animal figurines were not displayed in a way that showed they were important to her: They were everywhere, some of them piled on top of one another, and many still in boxes that she intended to unpack when she made room for them. Furthermore, there was really no selection process before she decided to purchase. When I asked her why she picked a particular one, she'd say it was "cute" or "different." When faced with the decision to purchase a new figurine, she didn't consider whether she had a place to display it or whether or not that particular figurine would add to her collection as a whole; she just gave in to the excitement of buying it.

She was an extreme case and clearly suffered from compulsive hoarding—she had a hard time parting with any of her figurines, and her home contained so many of them that it had become unlivable. The couches were covered with them; the kitchen counters were not usable; and the hallways had narrow paths in between the boxes these creatures came in. The living room and bedrooms were filled with unpacked boxes. The bed was usable, but she needed to push away a pile before going to sleep. In other words, her "collection" interfered with her life.

In less extreme situations, the line between collecting and simply amassing and accumulating is less clear. On the following page you

DO YOU HAVE A COLLECTION
OR A STOCKPILE?

Collection: Items adhere to a narrow theme—art deco jewelry, for instance, or Frank Sinatra albums.

Stockpile: The theme is ill defined or very broad (e.g., jewelry in general, old LPs).

Collection: Displayed in a careful manner that encourages viewing.

Stockpile: Untidy; gets in the way or prevents you from using areas of your home for their intended use.

Collection: Easily recognizable to an outsider as a special array of objects.

Stockpile: Just looks like lots of "stuff" to an outsider.

Collection: Is allotted enough room to be stored properly.

Stockpile: Items overflow in bins, drawers, closets, or piles.

Collection: Each item is unique and has special meaning.

Stockpile: May contain multiples of the same item.

Collection: Acquisition of items requires a strategy (for example, if you collect vintage coins, you may be saving up or searching to find one unique coin that completes your collection).

Stockpile: Items are purchased simply because you like them.

Collection: Collectors may belong to a community of other people who collect the same objects and are willing to swap and trade (as opposed to just getting and finding more).

Stockpile: Stockpilers gather things on their own and keep them.

Collection: You could give up an item in your collection if you need the money or the space for a better item.

Stockpile: You have a hard time parting with anything you've acquired.

will find a chart to help you get a better sense of whether you collect things or merely stockpile them.

SAVERS VERSUS PACK RATS

There's nothing wrong with saving things that you think you might need in the future, or things that might be of value. But there's a fine line between being smart and planning ahead, and saving anything that could conceivably be of use to you or someone else in the near future, which can lead to excessive clutter. Pack rats, as you may or may not know, are real rodents that are known for bringing all manner of twigs and grass back to their den, which is packed with little hovels and spaces for them to crawl around in. Their environment may make sense to them, but an outsider looking in would have a hard time imagining how that little creature could use all of that stuff.

Humans display similar tendencies. I've seen many cluttered homes with arguably "useful" stuff on the countertop, a drawer full of random odds and ends, or a cabinet teeming with food containers with mismatched lids saved from almost every take-out order the family has eaten. Saving supermarket grocery bags to be used as kitchen garbage bags makes sense, as does hanging on to a sweater that you rarely wear for the next time you go skiing, because it's perfect for that use, and you know you'll ski again at some point. And what about that silver tea set your grandparents left you, which has no particular sentimental value, and you never use, but you think must be worth something? Sometimes it feels like we should save things simply because they were given to us, not because they're meaningful or useful.

But in our society, where the supply of supermarket shopping bags is never ending and there are often far too many choices and things that are easy enough to acquire should you need them, when to stop saving (and when it might be wasteful to get rid of things) can be hard to figure out. Cassie had this very problem—she'd save gift

ARE YOU A SAVER OR A PACK RAT?

Saver: Can visualize a concrete use for something in the immediate future.

Pack rat: Will save anything that might be useful in the future or could theoretically be useful to someone they know.

Saver: Stops saving when he has enough useful items. (For example, you have enough grocery bags for the next week, at which time you are likely to get more at the supermarket, if needed.)

Pack rat: Has a hard time knowing when enough is enough and saves more than he can use; he thinks "it couldn't hurt" to save more grocery bags even though every time he opens the cabinet they fall out and need to be picked up.

Saver: Can get rid of something if it's clear she is not going to use it (such as an eyeglass case for glasses that are long since lost), even if it's potentially useful.

Pack rat: Will save an item that has outlived its utility, "just in case."

Saver: Will get rid of something if it's not used in a reasonable amount of time.

Pack rat: Loses track of how long he's had something until it becomes a fixture in the house.

Saver: Will discover he has two similar items and will choose the best one rather than saving both.

Pack rat: Will save multiple versions of the same item because "you never know."

wrap and other things that were technically reusable, but she saved far more than she needed or could use. Jason, too, struggled with this: While some of the appliances he collected were still usable, most people would not want a stained mixer bowl or a rusting toaster, even if it still performed the function for which it was made. Let's say Jason got around to rehabbing the computers he planned to. Not many people would be interested in purchasing a computer from the late 1980s, even if it worked, for a number of reasons. Jason did not use any of these things himself, so technically, they had no value. Yet it felt wasteful to him to discard them.

SENTIMENTAL SOUVENIRS

Souvenir shops line the most famous boulevards in the cities we visit, and most theme parks and museums have a gift shop tantalizingly located by the exit, making it likely that we'll stop in and buy something to commemorate our special experience. (*Souvenir* means "to remember" in French.) Many people don't feel as though the trip was complete unless they bring home a refrigerator magnet or a T-shirt to recall the memory.

But souvenirs aren't always items that are collected on trips. Henry, a young man I treated years ago, held on to every gift that his grandparents ever gave him. He feared that once they passed, he would forget the close relationship they had, so he would save things such as an outdated cell phone, holiday cards, empty packages that gifts came in, scraps of paper on which an unimportant note was written, and even socks that were now tattered with holes.

Out of habit, some people save bits and pieces from most every experience, not just the meaningful ones, and still others equate holding on to an item with holding on to a memory or a feeling—it's as if they didn't have the experience unless they keep the item. It's easy to see how your space can get so filled with stuff from your past that it's hard to live in the present.

Of course, what constitutes a worthy souvenir is subjective, and one person's important memory certainly may not have sentimental value to another. I have treated people who have held on to paper cups because a loved one who died had used them. It seems unusual when someone is saving everything a loved one had ever used, or when someone is saving something peculiar, like a disposable paper cup, but the principle is pretty common. I took a drink stirrer from a

ARE YOU SENTIMENTAL OR STUCK?

Someone who is sentimental is strongly motivated to act by emotions, and may hold on to things because of how she feels about them, rather than for practical reasons. There's nothing wrong with this, of course, except if you do it with too many things, which can create a clutter problem. If that happens, you may well be stuck. By that I mean that your emotions may serve as a paralyzing force rather than a motivating one— your feelings about your things take precedence over practical concerns.

Sentimental: You save something because you have a positive memory associated with it.

Stuck: You can't part with the souvenir even if it makes you feel bad (such as saving a mixed tape from the boyfriend you wish you'd never broken up with).

Sentimental: You save a few things that have positive memories associated with them.

Stuck: You save most everything with positive memories associated with them.

Sentimental: You save a few items that belonged to a person you care or cared about.

Stuck: You can't bear to part with anything that belonged to that person.

restaurant that my husband and I ate in every night on a cruise, just to remember the lovely experience. It's really not that different in theory, although I took one stirrer—not a stirrer, a coaster, a napkin, and a copy of the menu from every place we stopped. It's a matter of degree, of course.

Smith College's Dr. Randy Frost, whose research I admire and respect, has observed that some people with compulsive hoarding

Sentimental: You have a special place for your souvenirs.

Stuck: You pile your souvenirs in a drawer or closet that you rarely access.

Sentimental: You're capable of tossing something that has a positive memory if you need the space in which it's stored or you see that it has no use.

Stuck: You can't part with a special object no matter what.

Sentimental: You can get rid of the item after the memory stops being important to you.

Stuck: You save the item because the memory was once important to you.

Sentimental: You take good care of the things you save.

Stuck: The things you save get piled into the back of a closet, hidden under a bed, or stored in an attic or basement and possibly damaged by water or dust.

Sentimental: What you save honors an experience you've had or a person you knew.

Stuck: The saved item isn't particular to your own life experience.

issues might be more creative than non-hoarders, in that they recognize potential and beauty in more places than most people do. A twisted morass of wires and light fixtures could, with a little ingenuity and elbow grease, make a newly refurbished table lamp. If such visions are realistic, and the person actually gets around to making her vision a reality, we would refer to her as an artist. But if the person merely takes home the pile of metal and puts it on the counter, where it lives with dozens of other found objects collecting dust, that person may well have a problem with hoarding. The same principle may be at play here with sentiment. A person who hoards may feel more deeply about the items she brings into her home, as well as sentimental about more numerous and varied objects. Again, it's all along a continuum and becomes a problem when the sheer number of items begins to interfere emotionally and physically with your life.

Saving items for sentimental reasons doesn't always have to do with a memory per se. There are things we own that simply evoke an emotion, such as a bright blue hat that you don't wear but makes you happy to look at for no other reason than its color. But there are some who take it a step further: Not only do their possessions evoke a particular feeling, but, like Jennifer's feeling that she'd let down her Barbie dolls by allowing them to get ruined, they attribute human emotions to the items. One woman I know, who is not a compulsive hoarder, told me she recently emptied her closet of some 50 commemorative T-shirts she'd collected from races she'd run. She never wore them—they were big, boxy men's T-shirts—but she hated the thought of throwing away the memories of the races she'd completed. Frustrated by her limited closet space, she finally decided to make more room for the clothing that she actually wore, and got rid of all of the shirts except for the few she'd collected at marathons she ran. These were her crowning achievements, the ones she most wanted to remember.

WASTE AND ENVIRONMENTALISM

The concept of waste—"It would be a waste to throw that away"—is one that my patients struggle with mightily, as do many of us, particularly these days, when reduce/reuse/recycle is a way of living responsibly. Besides, we all want to feel that we've made the best use of an item we could, especially if we spent money on it. If we didn't use it thoroughly and thoughtfully, it would be a double waste, both of our hard-earned cash and of the item itself.

But there are many ways to be wasteful, and not all of them are as straightforward as throwing something perfectly good into the trash can. It may feel wasteful, for instance, to toss old notebooks that have some blank pages left in them, so you keep them. But they sit on the shelf looking sloppy, with shreds of perforated paper sticking out of the spiral. They are eyesores, and if you're not using them, they are wasting space that could be used for something else that actually is useful. You tell yourself you're saving them for the day your grandkids come over and need paper for coloring and doodling, but your grandkids would rather play video games than sketch in your old notebooks.

So is it truly a waste to get rid of the notebooks? Recycling is an option, as is donating them to a school, for instance. But if you're never going to get around to doing that (to recycle them, you'd have to tear the pages out and dispense with the metal spiral), the notebooks cluttering up your desk and the self-recrimination involved for not doing something more productive with them is a waste in itself. This is emotional clutter, on top of the physical clutter.

I know a family that kept a playhouse in their yard long after the kids had outgrown it. The couple didn't know what to do with it— they didn't feel it was clean and new enough to give to another family, but it felt wasteful to just put it out with the trash. So it sat in their yard getting dirty and slimy with rain and mud. Could it be used for something else, they wondered? They batted around ideas, but never really settled on anything. It was a classic case of how hard it is to answer the question: When is it wasteful to get rid of something that in theory could be used for something else? Throwing out the playhouse felt wasteful to them.

But if you reframe the situation, they had a beautiful backyard that could be used for another purpose, and they were wasting that space and opportunity by having a big old plastic playhouse lying fallow. What's more, the couple spent time and energy debating the playhouse question. It was a waste of their emotional energy to do that, at least, and at most, the playhouse may have been a reminder of yet another thing on their to-do list: figure out what to do with the playhouse! Multiply the playhouse example by a dozen or more other such decisions, and that's how much time and energy is wasted on excess stuff each month or year, depending on how much you own.

Add the worthwhile desire to be environmentally conscious into the mix and the decision-making process—to throw or to save or to redistribute through donation or recycling—gets more complicated. We hear so much about overcrowded landfills and recycling and reuse, and of course there's too much garbage in our disposable society. It makes it very difficult to throw anything away that's not rotting or utterly useless, even if you have no plans to use it. But is it any better to treat your home or your yard like a landfill? Instead of throwing away excess things, we simply keep them, store them, stockpile them, and only very occasionally use them. The end result is a house full of clutter, and that, too, is a waste.

And of course the biggest waste that comes from "not wasting" is when a person is harmed as a result of having too many things. Barry, whom you met with his wife, Melissa, was terribly depressed. His back injury kept him from working, and so he spent an excessive amount of time watching TV, but the fact that he couldn't get up and move around his house might well have made his physical problems worse. Being

IS IT A WASTE?

There are many ways to be wasteful, and sometimes the most obvious way—to throw something away that still has use—is actually less wasteful than the alternatives. If you're debating whether or not parting with a specific object would be wasteful, read through the criteria below.

It is a waste if . . .

☐ The item sits around your house unused. (A free thing sitting unused is a waste, even though you didn't spend money on it.)

☐ It takes up valuable space that could be used for something else.

☐ You devote more than a brief period of time to considering what you will do with it, which is a waste of your time.

☐ It overwhelms you to see it sitting there, which is a waste of mental energy.

☐ When you look at the item, you're reminded that you've avoided doing what you meant to with it—more mental energy wasted, and you wind up feeling bad.

☐ You buy more than you need in order to get a bonus of something you don't need—you waste money buying an item that will ultimately be wasted.

---

isolated certainly added to his emotional problems, and was not healthy for his body either.

It's very hard to accept the idea that not everything we have will be used, and that some of it will, necessarily, be "wasted." It makes people terribly uncomfortable. Some of us feel as though we are being ungrateful for all that we have, because after all there are people in the world who have much less. By not valuing what we have, the logic (which is of course not logical at all) goes, we do not care about those people who have less. Are we frivolous and impulsive?

Will others see us as such? All of these negative thoughts and distortions swim around in a person's mind when they consider getting rid of things, and lead to the anticipatory anxiety and fear of letting things go.

Factor in the symbolism that we associate with our things (discussed in detail on page 51), and the idea that our possessions may not be used to their full potential means that much more is wasted than the actual item. We've all had dinner with folks who consider any food left on a plate to be wasteful. Many of us heard from our parents that there were children starving in Africa, so we needed to be grateful for what we had and not waste it. The implication is that we selfishly took for granted that we were lucky, when the truth was, we were simply full or had been given too large a portion. The food represents the money spent on groceries, the time spent to prepare it, and perhaps even the love and care that went into making the food. To leave it on the plate feels wrong, and in some families, a child is made to feel like a bad person—a wasteful person—if anything is left uneaten. But is it any less of a waste to overeat when you're not hungry? Not really, and the stress that goes into "not wasting" is wasteful in itself. Eating food when you're not hungry may mean that you gain weight, which can cause you health problems that can waste your energy and your money as well.

———

In short, you don't have to be someone who is far along on the hoarding continuum, like many of the people I treat in my clinic, to be missing out on the kind of life you want and deserve to be living, on account of your relationship to your things. While you may not be living in physical peril, you may not be living comfortably either, let alone enjoying the life with your family that you work so hard for. Physical clutter yields emotional clutter, which gets in the way of your enjoyment and can be very stressful.

The good news here is that if your cluttering is impacting your life in a negative way, it is possible to change the way you think, and consequently change the way you interact with your stuff, which will result in a less cluttered environment. One common thought distortion I encounter with clutterers is, "I'm just a disorganized person, so there's no point in trying." This is a thinking error that holds many people back from reducing their physical and emotional clutter. When I treat people who have these thoughts, I help them to look around and recognize that it's probably not true, and replace that belief with a more helpful way of looking at things: "There are areas of my house that are not disorganized, and therefore labeling myself as disorganized is not an accurate statement."

Changing the way you think changes your behaviors, which further reinforces a belief system that will keep you on the right track. This is the basis of cognitive behavioral therapy (CBT), which has helped many people with compulsive hoarding and is equally effective in those with a less extreme problem. With CBT, small changes yield big results, which are rewarding in themselves and help you to perpetuate your positive behaviors. You'll find ways to do this in the coming chapters.

CHAPTER 5

WHEN IT'S TIME TO
TAKE CHARGE

IT'S A BIG DECISION TO FINALLY free yourself of the physical and
emotional clutter that's likely been occupying space in your life for too
long. For people who are far along on the continuum, paring down clutter can involve a concerted effort to change distorted thinking patterns.
For those on the mild end of the spectrum, and for those who have more
discreet problem areas (financial documents, for instance), getting a
handle on clutter can come about through developing new habits, ones
that are surprisingly painless to maintain. Either way, the payoffs—in
terms of feeling happier, calmer, and more in control of your environment, as well as improved relationships with friends and loved ones—
are enormous.

As mentioned, compulsive hoarders experience tremendous anxiety when confronted with the prospect of not being able to acquire a
desired item or having to let go of one or more of their possessions.
But non-hoarders with cluttering issues also experience a degree of
anxiety when faced with the prospect of cleaning out a closet or forgoing what appears to be a great deal. The suggestions I will offer in
the pages that follow are based on the treatment for anxiety disorders
that I offer at my clinic, through cognitive behavioral therapy (CBT).
When applied and practiced consistently, these methods can be
extremely helpful.

TREATMENT FOR COMPULSIVE HOARDING

When a new client visits my clinic for an evaluation, I begin by building rapport and trust with each individual. Many people who hoard do not seek treatment for their problem due to shame, embarrassment over the condition of their home, or fear of having to give up their possessions. It's very important that the client feels supported and respected in this process.

Through direct questioning and assessments, I can develop an understanding of the severity of the problem as well as determine the best treatment modality. More specifically, I ask the client to complete a biopsychosocial history questionnaire, which covers all aspects of his or her life, past and present. This includes but is not limited to childhood history; trauma or abuse history; comorbid diagnoses (sometimes there is more than one condition that factors into a patient's behavior, such as obsessive-compulsive disorder (OCD), attention deficit hyperactivity disorder (ADHD), or depression); family history of mental health issues; onset of symptoms and their impact on the person's life; medications the person is taking or has taken in the past; medical issues both past and present; current living situation; relational issues and so forth.

The next step is to augment this information with additional questionnaires, including one I developed, the Compulsive Hoarding Saved Items Questionnaire (see Appendix A), which identifies items people typically hoard and asks them to rate their anxiety level were they asked to give them up.

Because hoarding is a psychological condition that can be exacerbated by loss, stress, or other traumatic events, oftentimes in working one-on-one with my clients, we are able to identify triggers that led to the onset of the hoarding, which is important as we will need to address any feelings and issues that surface as we begin treatment. Together we also identify any environmental issues that played a part, such as growing up in a cluttered or hoarded home.

A key aspect in working with someone who is struggling with compulsive hoarding is to validate his struggles and to not blame him for his behavior or the condition of his home. It is quite likely that he has been yelled and screamed at by family members, and badgered, blamed, accused, and ridiculed for his hoarding. Understandably, family members become tired and fed up because of the stress and toll the behavior takes on them, which may include financial costs as well. Angry tactics are not going to motivate someone to get help, however. With understanding, compassion, respect, and open communication, we can work together to form an alliance to begin addressing the problems associated with their loved one's compulsive hoarding.

I also pose additional questions to my clients about how they live and their familial and social relationships, such as those noted below. If you are a clutterer, you might find it helpful to ask yourself these same questions.

How has the clutter or hoard impacted your life?

What spaces in your house are not usable for the purposes for which they were intended?

How is the clutter or hoard affecting the people who live with you?

If there are children present, do they invite friends over?

Do you invite guests over?

Do you feel emotionally attached to certain items?

Are you fearful that you will lose memories if you give up certain items?

Do you have any perfectionistic tendencies?

How do you feel your organizational strategies are working?

Do you have a hard time staying on task?

Do you have difficulty making decisions about what to keep and what to get rid of?

Are you afraid that if you give up an item, you will not be able to manage the anxiety you may feel over the loss of it?

If there were a fire in your home, what would you take with you?

If you were burglarized, what would be the worst thing that you would imagine could be taken from you?

In the beginning of treatment, I educate the client (and family, if indicated) on the condition of compulsive hoarding and the prescribed treatment protocol. In the initial interview, I assess any safety concerns to ensure that the home is not posing a health or safety hazard to the client or his family. Together we will establish goals and timelines that are realistic for the client, and discuss some of the decluttering rules. We discuss what's to come, including homework assignments designed to help him practice the decluttering process at home. This helps the client to apply the techniques without the assistance of a therapist to build his confidence that he can utilize the strategies to start making good decisions on his own.

Next, we schedule appointments for the client to begin bringing items into the office that he is willing to confront and challenge. In these sessions, he describes how he acquired the item, what it means to him, and why he is having difficulty letting go. We will work on thinking more realistically about these items and work toward making decisions about what he is willing to discard. Later in the process, I encourage my client to allow me to visit his home, which provides me with a clear picture of the degree to which he is hoarding and the work that needs to be done.

CBT AND HOARDING

Cognitive behavioral therapy (CBT) for compulsive hoarding is aimed at decreasing clutter, improving decision-making, and strengthening resistance to the powerful urges to save excessive stuff. More specifically, it is a set of strategies that focus on the factors that maintain the hoarding problem. Some of the strategies address the maladaptive beliefs and assumptions that compulsive hoarders have about themselves or their stuff, and other strategies are behavioral in nature, such as learning to resist a purchase, or letting go of the things that are causing the clutter. Still other strategies address problems related to time management, categorization, or organizational difficulties that interfere with one's ability to keep the home in order.

Cognitive behavioral techniques encourage you to take both a thoughtful and active approach to the negative thinking patterns that can fill your mind. This means confronting the distortions by challenging them and responding in a way that helps you to feel better about yourself. Most people have thoughts about themselves that are disapproving, pessimistic, and even harmful, and if they repeat them enough times, they'll come to believe these thoughts. Without an internal voice to help you explore the possibility that some of these messages "might" not be true, you tend to accept them as if they are fact. Some people's self-esteem is deeply affected by these negative messages, and they might even experience an onset of depression. Others may simply not be aware of them and go through their lives believing their distortions without exploring their accuracy.

Take, for instance, the following example: If a client says, "I can't throw anything away," this is likely a cognitive distortion we refer to as all-or-none thinking. It is a very stark, black-and-white way of looking at yourself, something the client is reporting as truth that is in all likelihood not true. Needless to say, seeing your abilities in black-and-white terms doesn't leave a person with many options. A CBT therapist would talk with this individual to help her explore at least one item that she doesn't feel strongly about. This would immediately disprove her statement, introducing "gray" areas, helping the individual to see how the statement is a distortion, and a negative one at that.

The therapy would then focus on building upon the things she can let go of, point out how all-or-none thinking isn't serving her, and look at other examples where all-or-none thinking might be holding her back as well. A more common example of all-or-none thinking that many clutterers often wrestle with is, "I'm so busy that I'll never have time to organize my house." The use of the word "never" is quite often a sign of all-or-none thinking.

It's easy to see how continually making life choices based on false, negative beliefs about yourself could lead to great unhappiness. If a person believes himself to be incapable of making good decisions about his stuff, for instance, he is unlikely to believe anyone who tells him otherwise, and is unlikely to make the effort that would disprove his beliefs about himself. He continues to remain in a cluttered or hoarded environment and goes on believing his truth—that he's a bad decision maker. People who hoard compulsively have many thought distortions around the power of their possessions and what they believe they would feel if they were to stop acquiring or get rid of those possessions—distortions that they believe are the gospel truth—so they keep accumulating, until they are trapped by their things, sometimes literally. Clutterers experience many of the same distortions as compulsive hoarders, but the thoughts are typically less extreme and intense.

An important concept that clients learn in CBT is that our feelings and our beliefs don't necessarily represent reality. Imagine a time when you believed someone was angry with you, and felt terrible about that, only to find out later that she wasn't. Or when you felt certain you'd failed a test, berated yourself for it, and it turned out that in fact you did quite well. In the moment, it felt real, but it turned out not to be true. Most of us can find many examples of how what we felt or believed in the moment turned out to be untrue, or if not completely false, vastly distorted and certainly not serving us well. By identifying these unhelpful negative thoughts as distortions, and disproving them with evidence that does not support the distortion, over time, you can begin to reshape your beliefs and your behaviors, and feel better about yourself and your capabilities.

Another example that illustrates how powerful these beliefs can be, and how unaware we often are that they are distortions: I've heard many guilt-plagued women say some version of, "If I can't keep my home clean and organized, I'm a bad wife and mother." Of course, this is also an example of all-or-none thinking. The woman who thinks this way is making a judgment on her entire aptitude as a spouse and parent based on the mistaken belief that good wives and mothers must be good at housekeeping. Aside from all-or-none thinking, this distortion is also an example of "labeling" (you are "good" or "bad" when rarely are people at either extreme, and whether or not you're good at keeping house doesn't say everything about your fitness as a parent or spouse) and "should" statements (a "good" wife should be good at everything pertaining to the home). In therapy, I would help the woman with these distortions recognize them as such, and come up with new beliefs that serve her better. In this case, those beliefs might be, "Keeping a home spotless doesn't make me a good wife. Being loving to my spouse, caring about his needs, and being a supportive listener help me to be a good wife." Eventually, these more realistic statements replace negative ones, and the client feels better about herself.

COMPULSIVE HOARDING AND COMMON COGNITIVE DISTORTIONS

Starting on the next page is a list of some common cognitive distortions identified by David Burns, MD, adjunct clinical professor emeritus of psychiatry and behavioral sciences at Stanford University School of Medicine, and how people with compulsive hoarding issues tend to use them. You will notice some overlap.

1. *All-or-none thinking (also called dichotomous thinking):* You see things in black-and-white categories. If your performance falls short of perfect, you believe yourself to have failed. People who hoard commonly engage in this kind of thinking, reflecting versions of, "If I can't keep the entire house uncluttered, there's no point in trying," or, "If I don't buy it now, I'll never find it again." Another common distortion I hear is, "If I can't control my shopping habits, I am a total failure." Looking at just the first example for evidence that contradicts the distortion, I help the client to see that even though there is clutter in some areas of the house, there might be other areas where there is not.

She might say, "Yes, but . . ." and I'll ask her to focus on what I've just said for a minute, give herself credit for what she's been able to clean up, and understand that things don't need to be perfect in order for her to be happy. So tenacious are some of these distortions that it takes a lot of practice and perhaps more than one bit of evidence that disproves the negative distortion to help a person consider that simply because she believes it to be true doesn't mean it is. I might then ask her to reframe that thought: "I've done a terrific job decluttering the living room, and I have a reasonable plan to get to the other rooms over the next week." It's the same set of facts, but a different, less defeatist way of looking at it.

2. *Overgeneralization:* A single negative event seems to you a never-ending pattern of defeat. Someone who hoards might say, "I'm having trouble making decisions about what to let go of. I'm just an indecisive person. I can't make decisions about anything in my life." A way to reframe that, once the person recognizes this belief as a distortion, might be, "Making decisions about what to get rid of is particularly difficult for me, but I make good decisions about many other things, such as when to take my child to the doctor or how to handle a tricky situation at work."

3. *Discounting the positive:* You reject positive experiences by insisting that they don't count for one reason or another, and in ignoring your successes, you focus only on that which you haven't accomplished. Let's say you did extremely well organizing the bathroom. When someone congratulates you on it, you dismiss it as a fluke, not that you were dedicated, focused, and committed to getting the area in order. In a similar example, you focus on the guest room, which is still full of stuff, rather than acknowledging how you cleared the kitchen and are halfway through with the garage. If your spouse gives you a compliment on how well you did in sorting through a pile of newspapers, you say, "Well, there are still five more piles to get to." When someone is adept at discounting the positive, I ask that person to stay with the compliment for a minute, and give herself credit for what she did. The fact that there is more to do does not take away from the fact that she did something well. It's okay to take credit for an achievement, no matter how big or small.

4. *Mind reading:* You negatively interpret the thoughts or feelings of others, even though there are no solid facts that support your conclusion. You might determine that your spouse is disappointed in you, without verifying this. "My husband said that he thought I was making better decisions while shopping, but he really thinks I'm out of control" is a way a clutterer might misinterpret a statement, giving it a whole new, negative meaning. Or "He threw out something I wanted to keep because he's trying to control me." Verification is the best way to poke a hole in this distortion. Asking your husband what his intent was in throwing out the item might well reveal that he thought it wasn't of value, and simply failed to ask you how you felt about it. By opening these communication lines, you can begin to work together on the purging process and learn what is important to each of you.

5. *Fortune-telling:* The person anticipates that things will turn out badly and treats the prediction as an established fact. The anxiety that accompanies these dire predictions is called anticipatory anxiety. They anticipate that something bad will happen if they get rid of an item (someone's feelings will be hurt, or they'll need it), and to avoid that anxiety, they hold on to it. "If I don't buy this now, I'll always regret it" is something I hear very often from people who hoard. Of course, if they always end up buying the item, they never actually test whether or not their beliefs are correct.

6. *Catastrophizing:* You expect the worst possible outcome and respond to it as if your prediction will come true. It tends to lean toward a highly exaggerated conclusion. I had a client who could not part with a broken towel rack. He said he didn't want to give it up because although it was broken, and although he had other functioning towel racks, he might need it in the future. He was keeping it to prevent having to experience anxiety attached to the fear that if he did give it up and needed it in the future, he would be rendered helpless by regret. My job as a therapist was to help him see that a broken towel rack would not be useful to him, and if his current towel rack broke, he'd likely want a new one, not a broken one, to replace it. Eventually he could recognize this thought as a distortion.

7. *Emotional reasoning:* You assume that your negative emotions necessarily reflect the way things really are: "I feel it, therefore it must be true." Many people who hoard engage in emotional reasoning such as, "I feel like others are judging me, so they must be." The person might avoid having people over or asking for help, which leads to isolation and withdrawal. When someone is engaging in emotional reasoning, I gently encourage them to consider that they don't know for a fact that what they feel in the moment is true. Once a seed of doubt enters their mind, we can test out their theory by asking. Even if they can't verify what they believe to be true, just the idea that they might be wrong can lead to thinking and feeling differently.

8. *Should statements:* You try to motivate yourself with shoulds and shouldn'ts, as if you can't do anything without a punitive voice telling you to. "I should have been able to get rid of more stuff," or "I shouldn't have so much trouble when it comes to organizing." "Musts" and "oughts" are used similarly. The emotional consequence is guilt, and a perpetual feeling that you've failed. "I should be able to control my shopping," "I should be able to throw away things that are broken," and "I should be able to resist a garage sale" are all should statements that clutterers may struggle with. By recognizing these statements for what they are—distortions that compare you against an arbitrary standard that you're not ready to meet—you can learn to meet yourself where you are in your process. For example, "I have not yet developed the skill to resist garage sales, but will continue to work on it." Or, "I am still working on healthy ways to make decisions about what to throw away, and I shouldn't expect myself to know the right choice every time I am challenged."

9. *Labeling:* This is an extreme form of overgeneralization, in which instead of identifying an error in your thinking, you attach a negative label to yourself or others, such as, "I'm a loser." In treatment, I often ask clients to look to a set of rules that work for them designed to curtail acquisition. If a client broke one of the rules, she might label herself by saying, "I bought something on impulse today, therefore I'm a failure." In other words, she did not simply give in and buy the eye shadow that called to her, but she is a failure as a person because of this one mistake. Mislabeling involves describing an event or a person with language that is highly colored and emotionally loaded.

CBT takes time and repetition, but several studies by Smith College's Dr. Randy Frost and his colleagues have shown that it can be effective in treating compulsive hoarding, particularly when patients take care to stay with it and not slide into old habits, which include defaulting to the thought distortions. The patients who tend to do the best with CBT are the ones who keep up with their homework assignments following their sessions.

EXPOSURE AND COMPULSIVE HOARDING

Exposure is the behavioral component used in CBT to help those struggling with compulsive hoarding learn how to manage the negative emotions that inevitably surface when facing and confronting their fears. Take, for instance, a person who is willing to drive past a garage sale without stopping, resist walking into a store that reads "closeout," or pass on a wicker basket that his neighbor is discarding. It's quite likely that feelings of regret will surface, in addition to several cognitive distortions, which may include "There may have been a good deal at the garage sale and I'll never know"; "I missed my opportunity to go to the closeout and will never forgive myself"; or "I should have taken the basket. My opportunity is lost forever." These distortions will breed feelings of intense regret that I will ask my client to sit with. Typically, the feelings of doubt (not knowing what he missed) and fear (I'll never get over it!) are not as bad as he anticipates, and the exposure of passing on these opportunities will ultimately help to test his fear about what he might feel, and in the long run, will keep the clutter down in the house.

Another example of exposure is getting rid of an item, and then sitting with the anxiety a person feels when he endeavors not to retrieve it. The experience might be one of loss, feeling like he can never get it back and will forever be without it. It can be quite challenging, which is why I prefer to start the exposure process on an item that my client would not feel particularly anxious about giving up. As I did with Jason, I ask clients to rate how anxious they anticipate they'd feel on a scale of 0 to 10 (0 equals no anxiety; 10 equals potential panic; and 5 is the middle, an experience of moderate anxiety). If an item is on the low end, a 2 or a 3, I start there. Once the client learns that he can manage his anxiety, we will work through the lower-level triggers (items) until he is ready to move to the next level.

There are some therapists who believe in "flooding," which is to address the items that the client has high levels of anxiety about right out of the gate. The belief is that by asking the client to face his highest anxiety first, it makes dealing with the lower-level items much easier. While this can be true, I feel that there is considerable risk involved in doing exposure in this manner. The reason is that when we feel anxious, our nervous systems alert us to potential danger. We need to respond in one of two ways: fight or flight. If the exposure exercise that the individual is asked to do—giving up an item that he thinks he couldn't live without—results in too high a level of anxiety, there is a risk that the patient won't be able to manage the anxiety, will retreat, and will terminate therapy. By gradually and systematically exposing a patient to his triggers, you increase a person's trust in the process and potential for success.

The way in which exposure bolsters CBT is interesting. Think back to my client who is engaged in fortune-telling about the towel rack: He is certain he will feel unbearable anxiety if he gets rid of the broken towel rack he fears he may need someday. If he doesn't challenge that thinking, he'll never discover whether he is right or wrong about how he'd feel. But if he's encouraged to face that fear—to get rid of the towel rack and monitor how he feels—he's likely to discover that his anxiety is at a manageable level. His anticipatory anxiety is far greater than his actual anxiety, and so he can recognize his thought as a distortion and change his behavior. My client agreed to part with the towel rack once he recognized his thoughts about it as a distortion. He anticipated he'd feel a good deal of anxiety about getting rid of it and rated his anxiety at a 6. Fifteen minutes later I asked him how he felt. He reported his anxiety had decreased to a 3 and felt strongly that he wouldn't retrieve it from the garbage, which he did not.

The same principle can work with cluttering as well. Think about an intractable closet or area of your home, and the anxiety you feel when you imagine sorting through your things. Let's say your closet is full of work clothing you haven't worn in years, ever since you began to work at home. You have two or three suits that you like, and several others that were your last choices even when you did have to go to the office every day. Rate your anxiety when thinking about getting rid of those suits. It might be high, because the thought of getting rid of them brings up worries about the future: What if you do go back to work and don't have those suits? You'd have to spend money on something you already had, which would be wasteful, which might be interpreted as being a "bad" person. The thought of going back to work might bring with it its own anxiety that gets conflated with the anxiety about getting rid of the suits. It's much easier to place the suits back into the closet and close the door. But if you do get rid of them (say, donate them to charity), odds are the anxiety you actually feel will be much lower than what you anticipated you'd feel.

Repeatedly facing one's fears and learning to manage the uncomfortable feelings and thoughts associated with these fears allows anxiety to gradually fade away. It can make overwhelming situations, such as cleaning out the garage, seem more manageable, and in the case of people who compulsively hoard, help them make good decisions about what to throw away or acquire. It doesn't mean the fear will go away entirely, but rather than act on the fear, the person can learn to simply acknowledge the fear and make a better, non-fear-based choice.

Here's how I work with clients when I'm helping them in their homes: I will go through the rooms with them, and help them get rid of what they can. Usually we start with what clearly appears to be trash, such as paper products, cans and bottles to be recycled, and so forth. When I notice an object someone is keeping—such as one of the hundreds of old, stained, broken appliances Jason kept with the intent to rehab and re-gift—and there appears to be little or no reason that it needs to be kept, I will ask the person to rate his anxiety about parting with that object.

In working through the process with Jason, who saw value in all of his broken possessions, I challenged his distortions: first, that someone would truly want a rusted mixer or blender, even though it is theoretically usable. Second, that to spend time looking for the replacement part and, assuming he found it, spend lots of money to purchase it (because it was outdated, it would likely be expensive) is probably illogical when he could buy a new appliance at a lower cost.

Through recognizing his distortions, Jason was able to make better decisions about what to discard, and by clearing more room in his home, he made the space he needed to fix the appliances that were actually usable and desirable to someone. So as Jason systematically began to let go of the appliances that were truly not worth saving (the exposure), he sat with the anxiety he felt when he let them go and stopped himself from going through the Dumpster to retrieve them (the response prevention). He discovered that, in fact, his anxiety was not as high as he anticipated it would be.

THE GREATER GOOD PERSPECTIVE SHIFT

There's a concept that I have found extremely helpful in treating people with anxiety disorders, which I'd like to introduce at this point. It's not rocket science—I think of it as a pop-up window in the brain that can give someone a little extra incentive and strength to do the hard work toward reaching her goals. I find it comes in handy in any situation in which what you're doing in the short term is not going to lead you where you want to be in the longer-term, bigger picture of your life. In addition to my work at The Anxiety Treatment Center, I am cofounder with Jeff Bell of YourGreaterGood.com, an outreach program based on a concept that can be used as an adjunct to CBT and exposure and response prevention therapy (ERP).

The idea is simple, but powerful: At any given moment, when you are making decisions based on avoiding anxiety, it's helpful to tap into your "Greater Good"—a larger goal that can benefit you or others and that, in calmer moments, you feel is more important than simply avoiding anxiety. In doing that, you can reframe your decision making, so that you can opt for bigger, long-term benefits, rather than merely staving off your anxiety in the short term. The Greater Good is a version of keeping your eyes on the prize.

This way of thinking can be particularly difficult for people with anxiety disorders, or anyone, really, who has anxiety about particular things, as most of us do. People in a state of anxiety see the world differently in the moment than they would if they weren't feeling anxious; they are so worried about unknown future outcomes that they do things in the present to try to control the future, when in fact what they're fearing may never transpire, and what they're doing may not alter any future outcome. More important, they're not enjoying their experience in the present. Anything that will relieve the anxiety seems like the "right" answer in the moment.

That's because anxiety makes a person's world seem black and white, and so too are the "default" choices the anxious person weighs: There's "right" vs. "wrong," or "good" vs. "bad." As seen through the distorted lens of anxiety, "good" choices are those that reduce fear and alleviate doubt; "bad" choices are those that increase fear and introduce doubt. So, for example, when a compulsive hoarder is in a dollar store and sees inexpensive swim gear at the end of the summer, her first impulse is to grab packages of goggles and floaties, because they're "good deals" that can be used next summer. It's seen by the hoarder as a good choice because, in the moment, the person feels like she's achieved something—a bargain—and because she avoids thinking about what would happen if she didn't buy the swim accessories and didn't have them when she needed them, or needed to spend more for them next summer. The facts that there are 10 months until summer, she has no place to store the equipment, and she probably already has boxes of goggles and inflatable pool toys in her garage from the last five times she saw a good deal at the dollar store don't occur to her or don't seem important in the moment.

But to consider forgoing the good deal causes her feelings of doubt and anxiety (What if she never sees this deal again? What if someone else purchases the goggles, and when she changes her mind and comes back for them, they're no longer available? What if she can't find what she has at home amidst all the stuff saved from years past?), so she leapfrogs over feeling that unpleasant anxiety and buys the gear. Her anxiety-driven brain sees this as a good choice, meaning that it's one that helps her avoid unpleasant emotions. But of course, it's not a good choice, as it leads to further excessive clutter and money wasted.

Because compulsions (in the example above, to purchase, but the same goes for saving things) temporarily reduce fear and/or doubt, they are almost always seen by an anxious person as good choices. But they are only good for alleviating or avoiding anxiety in the moment or short term. They don't serve the Greater Good, nor do they let the anxiety sufferer live a calm life. By introducing the idea that there is a Greater Good to strive for—a purpose or a service that is more motivating than the fear and doubt that anxiety breeds—the person not only learns to acknowledge her anxiety, but to ultimately make more productive decisions, including those essential to overcoming hoarding.

The Greater Good concept can work to help those of us who don't have anxiety disorders per se. Think about the reasons you have clutter, or how you feel when faced with an afternoon of sorting through your closets. You just don't want to deal with it, for the most part. You'd rather be doing something more enjoyable than sitting on the floor deciding whether to keep a set of old golf clubs that you rarely use. Making decisions about our stuff can bring up anxiety, even if we're not struggling with hoarding.

Let's say you have a pair of sandals that you wore 2 years ago. They're not worn out, but they are not in style, either, or particularly comfortable. You haven't worn them in 2 years because you have better options. But to decide to throw them away is still hard because of the judgments you might place on yourself: I am being wasteful; I "should" just wear them because they're still good, and it's frivolous to want something new when you don't really need something new, to name just a few.

These are all examples of distorted thinking. As I highlight in this chapter, it's not wasteful to get rid of something you are never going to wear again. In fact, it could be seen as wasteful to keep it, because not only is it taking up valuable room in your closet (wasting space), it is keeping you from easily finding other things you need (wasting time and causing you stress) and could possibly be used by someone else (wasting an opportunity to help). But thinking about all of this is tiring and stressful in itself. Who wouldn't rather postpone the chore? I know I would.

That's when it's helpful to keep the Greater Good concept in mind. Not cleaning out your closet causes you more emotional clutter than pushing through the dread and doing it. Every time you open your closet and see those sandals, among dozens of other anxiety-provoking decisions not made, you feel a wave of exhaustion and stress, and close the door again. The shortest path (throwing the shoes back in the closet for another day) may seem like the easiest path, but in fact it makes things harder down the line.

The Greater Good in this case would be simple: to have a clean, organized closet that doesn't cause you stress, and perhaps makes more room for your spouse's clothes and cuts back on tensions between the two of you over that issue. Keeping your eyes on that prize can be motivating. What's more, going forward, maintaining the closet in the moment (say, by getting rid of something unwanted when you bring something new) will save you future afternoons organizing when you'd rather be out and about.

In the case of the pool toys buyer, if I were with her in the store, I might ask her as she stops, wide-eyed, to consider the purchase, "What are your thoughts as you look at this beach ball?" Her response might be something such as, "It's such a good deal, and I know that the kids would love it. If I pass this deal up now, the opportunity will be forever lost!"

I might then point out, if this was the case, that this year the kids didn't really use any swim toys because they were at camp, and that she told me earlier that she doesn't even remember what swim items she already has, because she can't find any of them. (Reminding someone in a nonjudgmental way of what she told you earlier, when not in an anxious state, can be a valuable way to call attention to thought distortions.) I would then point out that she is thinking in all-or-none terms by imagining that her opportunity will be "forever" lost, and that she is fortune-telling in predicting the future as well. I would challenge her to consider that it is possible that the opportunity could arise again. It is likely that she would agree with this logic.

If, however, she is still stating that she is not able to resist the compulsion to purchase the toys, I will ask what her Greater Good would be in not buying them. She might suggest that it will help to not add to the clutter, that she will have an extra few dollars to spend on something that is readily usable and that she needs (which would be a way of taking care of herself), and it will make her husband happy that she did not bring in more outdoor items at the beginning of the cold weather (this is a service to others). I will then suggest the Greater

Good to help her to resist the purchase and sit with her anxiety and see what actually happens.

One humorous story: I once had a client who came into my office who said, "I must not have the right chair in my home." I asked him what he meant, and he said, "I have sat in every chair I can find to sit with my anxiety and none of them feels right." I explained that "sitting" with the anxiety is not literal, as it is the idea of emotionally being able to challenge your anxiety by confronting it and not doing anything to relieve it. While you certainly can sit in a chair and do this, individuals can also do this while walking away from a purchase, driving home, and so forth.

The techniques I illustrated here are the basis for treating people who compulsively hoard, but they work for anyone about to make a decision based on anxiety. The thought distortions and the learned behavior that lead to cluttered environments and impulsive purchasing can be unlearned with practice, and the Greater Good—an easier, less stressed life—is within most everyone's reach.

CHAPTER 6

THE DESIRE TO ACQUIRE: PULLING YOURSELF OUT OF HUNTER-GATHERER MODE

YOU MIGHT BE SURPRISED TO learn that the thinking patterns of someone who struggles with hoarding are not all that different from what any of us think when we see a new pair of jeans or a new gadget we simply cannot live without (even though, of course, we can, and, given the size of our closets and our electronics collections, and bank accounts, many of us should). Our adrenaline starts pumping, our vision becomes laser sharp, and for a few moments, it's like a scene in a movie where everything goes dark and a spotlight shines on the object of desire, in this case not a lover but premium denim or an iPad. Neurotransmitters—the chemicals that relay messages from your brain to your nervous system—start flowing, and the gotta-have-it high compels you to take out your credit card.

Some experts believe the desire to acquire is hardwired in the brain, and to an extent that may be true. Many animals, of course, hoard food in anticipation of times of scarcity, and some anthropologists believe that hoarding might have conferred early humans some evolutionary advantage. Of course, now that we are fortunate to live in a culture of plenty, this instinct (if it is in fact an instinct and not a learned behavior) is maladaptive. We don't need nearly as much as we can lay our hands on.

Most of us—myself included, who really enjoys shopping—have the ability to recognize when we're in autopilot acquisition mode, and stop ourselves from buying or gathering or helping ourselves to free key chains or whatever the bank is giving away. We simply remind ourselves that we don't need the item, can't afford it, or have no place for it. When we can't or do not stop ourselves from acquiring and buy or take things we don't need, we reconsider our decision when we get home and sometimes regret it. The buyer's remorse we feel acts as a natural deterrent the next time we're faced with a similar temptation.

A person suffering from compulsive hoarding has a much more difficult time putting the brakes on his impulse to acquire—and regret, castigation from family members, or even major financial debt are sometimes not enough to outweigh the impulse. Aside from the powerful adrenaline rush and sense of pleasure and achievement that many of us might experience when we "score" a great deal or find something we like, some researchers believe the pleasure center of the brain may be stimulated during acquiring. Between the impulse control problem, the desire to avoid anxiety, difficulty making good decisions, and powerful cognitive distortions driving the acquisition, the person who hoards has much to contend with when faced with an enticing object. And if the person is inclined, like many non-hoarders are, to use shopping as an escape from the routine stresses of life, loneliness, or other emotional issues, their compulsion to acquire becomes even more powerful.

Sometimes a person who compulsively hoards will make a conscious decision to go hunting and gathering—shopping, visiting garage sales, or Dumpster diving—and other times he will simply be walking out of the movie theater, for example, and get drawn into a closeout sale across the street. Think of this person as you would someone whose immune system is compromised: He could be exposed to the same pathogens as anyone else (in this case, tempting sales) but is far more susceptible to picking them up and getting sicker than someone who had a healthy immune system to fight off disease.

RETHINKING HOW YOU SHOP

As I've said previously, among people who hoard, just as among non-hoarders, the drive to acquire varies in intensity. While acquiring and parting with items is something all people who hoard struggle with, some are particularly prone to the front-end of compulsive hoarding (i.e., they are fiercely driven to acquire), whereas others have greater difficulty getting rid of things.

I had a client named Toni who had a particularly strong compulsion to acquire. I worked with Toni and her husband, a man who is deeply devoted to her and badly wanted to help her with her hoarding problem. He was the breadwinner in their home, and she would spend her days until he got home from work shopping and staking out the best deals.

Most of her motivation to acquire stemmed from being a genuinely kind person, as reflected in her desire to give to and do things for others. Toni often went to discount stores, where she focused on the bargain section, and bought items she thought she'd give as gifts to people in the future. Sometimes she'd buy craft projects, such as needlepoint sets to make pillows for her friends' children, or stationery she thought she'd use to write thank-you notes to the many people in her life who had been thoughtful. She also purchased excessive amounts of clothing.

Walking into her house, I saw what I see frequently in hoarded homes: what I call the Target/Walmart/Home Shopping Network explosion. These outlets, with their low prices and temptingly arrayed merchandise, can be irresistible to people who hoard. Bags, gift tags, boxes, packages, and other piles of newly purchased items were carefully arranged into stacks and more stacks leading to the ceiling. Although an outsider would likely be unable to discern any rhyme or reason to these stacks, Toni knew exactly what was in each bag or box and what she intended to use it for.

Toni's husband, who would gently make suggestions about what to get rid of, would be met with a giggle and, "Don't be silly, that's for Mary," or, "No, I can't give that up. I'm going to use that for a church project." By the time I became involved, he felt that there was no point in making suggestions, because Toni would ultimately defend her intentions.

Toni, like many people who hoard, rarely got around to doing any of what she planned with the stuff she bought. During the day, while her husband was at work, she was scared she'd miss a good deal if she didn't hit the stores, and so was out most of the day. When her husband got home, she'd devote all her time to being with him, and they enjoyed traveling on the weekends to visit loved ones. Toni was also very social and involved in her community, something that those who hoard on the extreme end of the continuum sometimes have a difficult time with because they are isolated by their hoarding and embarrassed to have people over.

This, I believe, was in part why her husband was so tolerant. He wasn't at home that much and so was able to distance himself from the explosion of stuff in their house. Also according to her husband, Toni's attentiveness to him helped to make up for the way they were living. While Toni's love for her husband may have made it easier for him to live in a hoarded home, he feared confronting her, and that limited his willingness to set boundaries. It is critical for those living with someone who clutters or hoards to not simply adapt and accept the situation, but to continually assert his or her needs.

I started my work with Toni and her husband by asking her to turn over the credit cards to him, and to steer clear of certain stores that she had a particularly tough time resisting. She admitted she felt powerless against the urge to shop, and not having an easy way to pay placed an obstacle between her and a purchase. The couple was also in debt, so I asked Toni to carry a limited amount of cash and to avoid trips to the bank. This was strictly a short-term solution, however. While limiting access to acquisition can help in the treatment of compulsive hoarding, relying on avoidance long term means that the person never has the opportunity to learn how to resist her urges. I had Toni do these measures as a stopgap while we dealt with clearing out her home and developing a better understanding of her acquiring and hoarding behaviors. Eventually she would need to learn to manage having the credit cards and cash on hand and to resist impulsive purchases.

At first, Toni and her husband shopped together for what they actually needed, which had its challenges, because she could talk him into going into one of the off-limits stores "just for a quick peek," and he had a hard time denying her what she wanted. He said he just wanted her to be happy. One of the reasons I treat the whole family is that oftentimes those close to someone who hoards find themselves helping the person avoid anxiety in the moment, and lose sight of the long-term goals. Toni's husband was not yet able to see that in the long run, she would be happier by resisting acquiring, which would give them more space to sit on the couch and the ability to eat at the dinner table together, and so forth. This is an instance where appealing to Toni's Greater Good would have come in handy.

With this information, we formed a new plan and agreed that I would shop with her so that we could actively address her cognitive distortions as they surfaced when she was tempted to buy something she didn't need, which would help her to start to think differently during the acquisition stage. Our goal would then be to have her practice these newly developed skills with her husband.

What happened at the grocery store, where she and I began, was typical of every shopping trip we made. The store was arranged in a way that is particularly troublesome for a person trying to break her hoarding patterns: No matter which of the two entrances we used, the first thing we saw was the discount cart and Today's Specials. While it's all well and good to save money on things you truly need, for someone who is trying to stick to a list, what happens to be on sale that day is likely not on the list and only adds to the clutter. Reminder: It's not a "good deal," no matter how inexpensive it is, if you're not going to use it, if you already have another like it at home that will expire if you don't use it, or if it takes up space, which causes you stress.

Even though we had our list, Toni was insistent on doing a quick forage through the cart, which contained toys. She and her husband had no children, and she did not have a specific child in mind, but wanted to purchase various toys "just in case" she met a child who could use them. She followed the same pattern with food. Although there were items on special that she didn't particularly care for, she would want to buy foods because they were good deals, thinking that perhaps someone might stop by the house who might care for them. It's easy to see why her kitchen had no counter space. All the surfaces were covered with baked goods (which neither Toni nor her husband ate), cake mixes, and beverage containers, just waiting for company to stop by. She and her husband had to buy microwavable or prepared food from the supermarket because they had no room to cook. This tendency to "browse" for things that you didn't intend to buy and don't need is very common among clutterers as well.

Buying something "just in case" some unforeseeable future event takes place, or in case some unnameable person shows up and wants to use the item, is a common theme with people who are struggling with hoarding. For Toni, the thought of what would happen if she left the can of chili on the grocery shelf and someone came over craving chili was too anxiety-producing to think about, so she'd toss the can in her cart. It sounds highly improbable when I take it to its logical conclusion—the odds of a guest Toni couldn't name having a chili craving at the exact moment she was at Toni's house were extremely small—but in the moment, the anxiety felt very real, and she based her behavior on avoiding it. Non-hoarders, without thinking about it, also fill their homes with things that look like they may be of use to someone in the future, only to a lesser degree.

More than one cognitive distortion is often at play at the same time. In Toni's case, when I questioned her about her need to acquire so much food (especially food she and her husband didn't even like), she said, "What if someone comes by, and I am not prepared to serve them something tasty? That would make me a bad hostess." That is Labeling. I reminded Toni that she is discounting the other aspects of her ability to entertain a guest, and making a guest a cup of tea and serving it in a tidy, comfortable family room would be another option to consider, if someone stopped by.

Standing in front of the cart of toys, Toni would excitedly pick each one up and examine it from all angles, read what age child the toy was intended for, and talk about how cute it was. "Don't you think it's adorable, Dr. Robin?" she'd ask. I'd avoid answering that question. If I said "yes," then she would use my answer as a rationalization for purchasing it, and we might wind up in a circular conversation, with her defending the purchase. If you're shopping with someone with a drive to acquire, gently ask the person questions such as, "Do you have a use for that item—today?" And, "Do you have a home where it can live?" Oftentimes, the answer will be no to both questions. Instead, I asked her whom the toy was for. She replied, "Well, let me think . . ." and I could see the wheels turning as she went through the mental directory of every child she knew. For some of the toys, she would come up with a specific child, but most of the time she was able to admit that she wanted to get the toy "just in case" she met a child who could use it.

At this point I challenged her to think about what might be the Greater Good of resisting the purchase of the toy, which is something any clutterer might want to ask herself at the point of purchase. It was not her natural inclination to consider the long-term benefits of not acting on impulse, so she thought about it long and hard, and she finally said, "Resisting this toy would keep me on my path of trying to bring less into my home, and it would make my husband happy to know that at least for today, I was able to resist temptation." I was thrilled that she could apply the concept, and we moved forward, her head turning around to look longingly at the cart as we walked away. I didn't acknowledge that, but instead supported her for the good decision she had made. I told her that I would fully expect her to have a hard time, but she made the right choice, and that is what I wanted her to focus on.

It wasn't easy for Toni to walk away from the items she decided not to purchase, but after a while her mind did move on to other things, which I gently pointed out to her, so she could recognize that she would not be forever tormented by not buying them once she'd walked away. Such a strategy could be helpful to a clutterer as well: If you walk away from an object and allow yourself to feel your anxiety but don't act on it, you will find that most items do not rise to this level of importance. Toni found that she could forget about the items empowering.

The key here, for both Toni and a non-hoarder who nonetheless buys on impulse, is to question your fearful assumptions of what will happen if you don't buy the item, which requires slowing down and keeping presence of mind, rather than just buying the item by rote. It can also help to test your anxiety about what will happen if you don't buy an item (someone else will snap it up, I will regret not grabbing it when I could), and experience how the anxiety diminishes with time.

(continued on page 126)

THE BIGGEST SHOPPING TRAPS THAT LEAD TO CLUTTER

A frequent trap, or cognitive distortion, shoppers experience is the idea that they would suffer indefinitely for passing up a purchase, but there are others as well. I don't mean to suggest that certain items are never a good deal or worth buying even if they weren't planned for. The point is that if you have a clutter problem, some of these rationalizations to buy are often not accurate and can keep you trapped in a buying pattern that's not serving you.

The Trap: "It is such a good deal, I can't pass it up."

The Fear: If I pass it up, and I need the item, I will have to spend vastly more on it at another store. I might miss out on it altogether if there are no more left here when I come back.

Alternative View: It's only a good deal if you need it, have room for it, and are going to use it at a specific time in the (ideally near) future. You may never need it, in which case it might be considered a waste of money and space. You may also feel regret every time you look at it. If you do need to spend more on the same item later, the odds are fairly good that it won't put you in debt.

The Trap: "I might never find something like that again. You never know when you might need it!"

The Fear: I might be caught without something I need desperately, and that will feel terrible. If I don't have what I need, I don't know what I'll do!

Alternative View: If you can't identify why you need an item when you're purchasing it, it's likely that you don't currently need it. If you do need it in the future, you will find a way to get it or live without it. And you may never need it, in which case buying it was a waste of money. Living in the present with what you need now and for the immediate future is the key to a clutter-free life, and having faith that you can provide for yourself when you need things is something you can build with practice.

(continued on page 124)

THE BIGGEST SHOPPING TRAPS THAT
LEAD TO CLUTTER *(continued)*

The Trap: "This item is useful, so I should keep it."

The Fear: I am somehow wasteful if I don't try to make use of an item that is not, in my mind, completely useless. If I don't save an item that has potential use—let's say a pair of scissors that are too dull to use, but I have no idea where to take them to get sharpened and am unlikely to make a point of finding out—I anticipate the regret would be unbearable, and if I waste, it also means I am a wasteful person, which is the worst thing a person can be, given that some people don't have enough to eat.

Alternative View: It may have use, but if you don't have use for it in the moment, you are not going to make it any more useful by keeping it in a drawer. It is not wasteful to get rid of something you don't need. You are not responsible for making use of everything that crosses your path.

The Trap: "I'm getting it as a backup, just in case I need another one."

The Fear: If I find myself without something I need, I'm afraid I won't know what to do.

Alternative View: We live in a land of plenty. If you need another one of the objects in question, you can get it when you need it, or get something else that will work just as well. If you have a specific fear about a specific incident taking place (for example, the toilet keeps overflowing, and it is likely to happen again soon, and so it's a good idea to have a supply of paper towels on hand), that's worth considering. But preparing for an event with no foundation is another trap that will lead you to hold on to things you don't need.

The Trap: "I've had a rotten day and I deserve a treat."

The Fear: Buying something for myself will make me feel better, and I just don't have the energy to fight it; I think that it would cause me to feel worse if I don't buy something.

Alternative View: It's understandable that you'd want to do something nice for yourself after a hard day, but contributing to your clutter is the opposite of doing something nice for yourself—you're adding stress to your life, making it harder to find things, and spending money you may not have. Why not treat yourself to something nonmaterial, like a walk in the park or a phone call to a friend?

The Trap: "This would make a great gift for someone."

The Fear: Even though I don't have anyone in mind right now, I might encounter someone who could use it. If this were to happen, it would mean that I wasn't being thoughtful and considerate at the time that I could have made the purchase.

Alternative View: The item may make a great gift, and by leaving it in the store, you give another shopper the opportunity to buy it for someone. If you don't know whom you're giving it to, it's likely only going to sit in your home, unused and unappreciated. When you need a gift for a specific person, one will be available then. You can make the decision based on what that person's needs are, which is truly thoughtful.

The Trap: "My mom would never let me have things like this when I was a kid. Even though I may not use it, I just want to have it anyway."

The Fear: It made me feel so bad to not have control or the things I wanted when I was a kid that I'm going to exercise control now that I can.

Alternative View: Getting yourself what you weren't allowed to have as a kid isn't going to take away your sadness from feeling deprived of certain items as a child, and is only going to add to the clutter in your house. Acknowledge that you could have it if you do want it. You have that control now.

The Trap: "It's an amber necklace, and I collect amber jewelry. I have to have it!"

The Fear: If I don't get this particular necklace, I will miss out and regret it. I will look at my jewelry collection and think, "If only I had bought that . . . "

Alternative View: View your collection as an opportunity to be creative and thoughtful. Don't just purchase an item because it represents a category, but look at the style, theme, artist, and so forth. How different or special is it compared to the items you already own? All of that information will allow you to make a considered decision.

THE ALLURE OF THE FREE AND THE CHEAP

People who compulsively hoard, as well as non-hoarders with a clutter problem, do not only acquire their stuff at stores. There's something about items being given or thrown away, or sold for cheap at a garage sale, that entices many people to collect objects they don't need.

Many people get a different kind of satisfaction when foraging at secondhand venues or through discarded items, versus buying new. Most obviously, items are cheaper, and so the perception of value is heightened at a garage sale or flea market. Occasionally the seller will share the history of the item—the jelly jar glasses belonged to an aunt who lost her parents at a young age and was taken in by strangers, and so the glasses were special to her. For a hoarder, who is already predisposed to have heightened sentimental attachments to physical things, stories like this make an item all the more enticing. The fact that the item is being sold at a garage sale also increases a hoarder's sense of urgency in acquiring the item—if I don't take it now, I will never have the opportunity again, because the garage sale will be over and I can't come back.

The sense of personal fulfillment and satisfaction that those who compulsively hoard get from "rescuing" items that others consider useless cannot be overstated. Many hoarders feel a sense of excitement and accomplishment by imagining themselves doing what others could not do: finding a use and value in what is, to most of the world, disposable. It isn't that a hoarder believes he is better than the person who threw away the item, but he can sometimes exhibit a sense of grandiosity—a belief that he can accomplish what others cannot, such as building something spectacular out of nothing.

This unrealistic sense of what they can achieve, some vague time in the future, with the right items, when they have the time, is part of the cognitive distortions that contribute to a compulsive hoarder's volume of possessions. Many feel a sense of optimism about what they can and will accomplish that is completely disproportionate to reality. Recall Jason, the garage sale fan who collected broken appliances, or Trevor, with his outdated computer parts taking over the guest room, or even Toni, with her crafts projects for others that she never had time to complete because she was so busy shopping. Their intentions are good, but are rooted in many distortions in their thinking and mental traps. Letting go of what these discarded and unloved items represent for them (achievement, creativity, generosity) is typically harder than not acquiring the item in the first place. Where there is stuff, there is always potential, is the idea. If you look at the world through their eyes, it's easy to see why buying or acquiring beats the alternative.

Free things pose an even greater, if somewhat different, challenge to hoarders and clutterers alike. The idea of getting something for nothing, and often something new (a sample or promotional item) rather than secondhand, is hard to resist. I travel a lot, and I admit that I have a hard time leaving behind the free shampoos from the hotel room, even though I have my preferred brand that I buy whenever I need it (and also travel with it). I'm not going to use the tiny bottles of shampoo, but feel somehow that I'm getting my money's worth if I take them—I paid for the room, after all. I also don't like missing out on a "free gift" period at the Estée Lauder counter. I use their face powder and wait to buy it until they offer the free gift, usually a makeup bag with some samples. I don't use the makeup bag, but I love the idea of the free gift. It makes no sense, and yet at the time, it seems to make perfect sense. Why would anyone buy something *without* the free gift, when they can buy it *with* the free gift? Personally, I am able to resist things that I don't have room for, but for the person who struggles with clutter or hoarding, passing up free things can be a major challenge.

Dorothy Breininger, one of the personal organizers with whom I work on *Hoarders* and the president and founder of the Delphi Center for Organization in Los Angeles, has a wise saying: "Free can be very costly." What she means is that freebies—those bottles of shampoo, that airplane sleep mask, or the little nail file with the corporate logo at the realty office—cost you in terms of clutter and the stress it can lead to. Clutter in your car, in your handbag, in your office, or in your home creates unnecessary stress because you are unable to find what you need when you need it; important things like receipts and bills get mixed in with all the other stuff and can cost you money if you lose them; and you can miss out on important events, unearthing a baby shower invitation a week after the event has passed. Clutter can also make you feel bad when you see it, because it reminds you of a chore—cleaning up—that provokes anxiety.

NO ADMITTANCE! FIVE WAYS TO AVOID BRINGING CLUTTER INTO YOUR HOME

According to personal organizer Dorothy Breininger, it's best not to bring things into your home in the first place, unless you really want and need them. "Once they're in your home, you get attached to them and it's a lot harder to get rid of them, even if you don't need them," she says. I agree. Here are five ways to avoid bringing more clutter into your home.

1. Don't fall for freebies. Free things are rarely free, and cost you big in terms of clutter, disorganization, and even money.

2. Shop for your goal. If you have a cluttered home, pick one area that you consider your indulgence, and direct your purchasing there. If you like to travel, for instance, remind yourself of the trip you're saving up for the next time you're trying to resist an item in an antiques store. Wouldn't you rather spend that money on an unforgettable dinner in a beautiful vacation spot? Ask yourself whether you need another set of candlesticks or other items that may clutter your kitchen table. This is a variation of the Greater Good: Remember your long-term goal to resist impulsive shopping.

On a practical level, those free shampoos take up what Dorothy calls prime real estate. You unpack them from your travel bag and put them on the counter, where they create clutter, making it harder to get to the things that have a permanent home there, like your toothbrush and face cream. So you move them into the medicine cabinet, where they block the Tylenol, and so when you have a headache and look for it, you need to dig, knocking all the shampoos and eye drops and other sundry items into the sink. You eventually become frustrated and annoyed, all because of something that was supposedly free. Clearly, those shampoos were not free at all. They

3. Shop the perimeter. At supermarkets, drugstores, and big-box retailers like Target, the items you truly need are usually in the outer aisles of the stores. If you need something specific from the inner aisles, venture in, but don't just browse for fun.

4. Stick with your brand. As Dorothy points out, we're faced with too many choices of similar items. If you like your Blackberry, there's no need to "try out" the iPhone just because your friend has one. You probably won't like it any more than the device you already own, and you'll be faced with the learning curve of a new piece of technology as well as a bunch of new boxes and chargers and travel adapters that add clutter to your house. (If you have a good reason to switch, by all means, switch, but not just for the heck of it.)

5. Give away gifts. You don't need to keep something just because it's a gift. Especially after a big event like a wedding, graduation, or birthday, go through the presents you've received and decide what to do with them: keep, re-gift, return, or donate. If you get a CD that you know you won't listen to, don't store it with the rest of your CDs, says Dorothy. Put it by the door with the gift receipt taped to it and exchange it, or re-gift it as soon as possible. Once it's in your home, it will be mixed in with the clutter. Better yet, let gift givers know in advance what you like.

cause you stress and cost you energy that would better be used for something else.

What's more, as Dorothy says, free things are rarely truly free, even in a monetary sense. She cites the following situation many of us find ourselves in: Let's say you sign up for an offer of three free issues of a magazine. Naturally, the company requires a credit card, which will not be charged unless you "decide to" continue your subscription. Few of us make an active decision to continue the subscription; we simply forget to cancel it, or forget to even consider whether we want to continue it. So you do nothing, and the magazine keeps coming, and you begin to pay for it. If you were about to sign up for a subscription to the magazine anyway, that might be fine, but odds are, you were hooked by the three "free" issues.

Since you didn't actively want the magazine in the first place—you didn't say to yourself, "I'm going to sign up for *Boating and Skiing* today," but the three free issues made it hard to pass up—you're probably not reading it, and it becomes another thing cluttering your house, and another thing you feel guilty about because it's a waste of money to get a magazine you're not reading. That stack of magazines you're not reading becomes emotional clutter. You may want to stop the subscription, but you're not sure how to do so; you probably needed to have saved a special code number from when you signed up and have no idea where it is. So you spend more than an hour calling various 800 numbers and entering your information into a computerized phone system to try to cancel your subscription, which is extra complicated because it was a special promotion through an outside company, and you begin to feel tense and angry. Perhaps you give up, and since the magazine is on auto-renew, you continue to receive it for years to come. Stopping the subscription remains on your to-do list along with all the other projects and tasks that you intend to get to. All because you went in for what sounded like a freebie.

Even free in-home services can add to your emotional and physical clutter, Dorothy notes. Let's say you have someone come to your home to perform a "free, no obligation" assessment of your heating system. Soon you are receiving aggressive and prolific junk mail from

DR. ROBIN'S RULES FOR CLUTTERERS

Rule #1: One in, one out. If you buy a pair of shoes, you must have a pair in mind that you're going to discard or donate, to prevent closet overflow.

Rule #2: No homeless items. If you're considering bringing something into your home, you must be able to identify where it will live or what it will replace. "In the hall until I find a place for it" is not an answer you should accept from yourself.

Rule #3: Be able to identify how and when you are going to use the item. In addition to a home, the item needs a plan. "Oh, cool, a tub of modeling clay on sale—what a good deal!" isn't a reason to bring it home. "Next weekend my nieces are coming over, and they'll enjoy making things out of clay" is a good reason. Note that there is both a date and a specific project in mind for the item.

Rule #4: Do things in the moment. If you purchase a new sweater and know you need to get rid of one, pick that sweater in the moment as you put the new one in the closet. If you put it off, you're unlikely to ever get around to choosing one to get rid of.

Rule #5: No duplicates. If you already have an item, buying another one just like it is not a good idea, even if it is a good deal. The exception is if you have a storage area devoted to such items, like cleaning products in the basement. However, there must still be a clear plan about when or how you are going to use it.

Rule #6: If it needs to be fixed in some way, it doesn't come in. Far more often than not, you won't get around to repairing it. If you're trying to cut back on clutter, nothing broken or in need of refurbishing should cross your threshold.

that company, and sometimes phone calls and e-mails, all of which clutter up your mailbox, your home, and your computer. If you don't succumb to the sales pitch (and companies that offer free trials don't give up easily because you've already demonstrated an interest), you need to spend hours of your time deleting e-mails and removing yourself from their mailing lists. Even if you need the service that the company is offering, the allure of the freebie often blinds you to whether the entire package is a good value.

In short, "free" things are usually best avoided, especially if you have an issue with clutter. People who are highly organized and do their research and comparison shop may well benefit from services like these, but companies tend to capitalize on those who aren't, despite their best intentions, organized.

Shopping for Something You Cannot Buy

Some people use shopping as a means of feeling a sense of personal fulfillment, as well as a way to avoid addressing some of life's more painful realities. You may recall Amanda, the young woman who lived with her parents, didn't work or have many friends, and filled her days with shopping from home. She is the perfect example of this very common tendency among those who hoard as well as those who don't.

Once Amanda was able to control her spending, she was able to recognize that there was more to life than shopping and isolating herself from the world in her bedroom. But you don't have to have a problem with hoarding to use shopping as a means of avoiding difficult feelings or issues in your life. The act of hunting down an item and making it yours is thought to stimulate the chemical pleasure center in the brain, and can leave you feeling a sense of accomplishment, even if it is fleeting. There is a comfort for many people in buying new things, and the social aspect of getting out of the house and becoming part of the crowd at a mall or shopping center can be very appealing. Shopping is mindless and easy, and our desire to acquire beautiful things is a natural impulse. When our lives are emotionally challenging, we can sometimes feel the need to surround ourselves with beautiful objects. It doesn't ultimately fulfill the inner need, but it can be a distraction, at least for the moment.

Unfortunately, it's that very distraction—that temporary hit of pleasure and relief from the pain or discomfort that you're feeling— that makes you want to return to the mall for more. And the more a shopper distracts herself with shopping, the less likely she is to sit with the feelings she's trying to avoid, and let those feelings pass through. The harder road—the one that leads to the Greater Good of the life you want to live—is to face those uncomfortable feelings. Whether it's anxiety, sadness, grief, loneliness, or depression, we can only get past our pain when we address what's causing it. Retail therapy is not the answer.

Below is a list of activities that I encourage clients to consider doing when the urge to shop strikes. By doing something else, something that may not provide the same escapism but can help you feel better, you'll be truly improving your life, rather than just adding to the clutter. Changing your behavior can help you change the way you think too—that's one of the principles of cognitive behavioral therapy.

> • *Exercise.* If you shop when you feel down, go for a brisk walk, run, or do another activity that gets your heart rate up. Exercise helps you work off excess adrenaline and elevates the levels of feel-good chemicals in your brain. Yoga, likewise, can have a calming and centering effect. Any amount or kind of movement is better than none.

> • *Meditate.* Meditation can decrease anxiety. You don't need to take a formal class. Simply closing your eyes, breathing deeply, and repeating a comforting mantra to yourself can help.

CLUTTER-INCREASING SHOPPING TRICKS WE ALL FALL FOR

It's a rare person who is immune from some of the techniques marketers and retailers use to try to get us to buy more than we need. If you have a problem with clutter, you may be particularly susceptible to these techniques. Here are a few to be aware of, so you're not caught opening your wallet in a moment of weakness.

☐ **Free shipping.** When ordering online, it's tempting to order more than you had intended in order to qualify for free shipping, but do the math before clicking. Let's say you're buying a book for $20, and spending $5 more would get you free shipping; so you add a $10 book you don't really need and probably won't read to your basket. You've just spent more than you would have had you just paid for shipping, and have doubled your clutter potential.

☐ **Black Friday sales or any major holiday weekend sales.** You can certainly get good deals at these events, but their chaotic atmosphere prompts many people to make poor decisions and buy more than they need. Limited-time sales create a false sense of urgency and foster competition between shoppers, which adds to the sense that there is value in what you're competing for.

☐ **Large shopping carts.** When you can, use a handbasket when you go to big-box stores like Target, rather than a giant shopping cart, which you'll be tempted to fill with things you don't need. If you truly need lots of stuff, let your spouse or shopping partner carry a basket, too, or place two baskets inside a cart and don't buy more than can fit into those baskets.

☐ **Mirrors everywhere.** Most clothing stores are furnished with mirrors on the walls, and odds are when you see your reflection, you're likely to find fault with it—and reach for something on a rack to make you feel better. Just like it's never a good idea to go food shopping when you're hungry, it's important to take the time to wear something that makes you feel attractive and confident so you're less likely to feel the need to "fix" yourself with a new outfit.

• *Go to a café or to the library* instead of the mall. The social aspect of shopping is a big draw, but you can get that in a more meaningful way by meeting a friend for coffee or taking your child to a storytime hour. You could also go to a bookstore that's hosting a free author event, or a knitting store that offers free classes. Just be sure to leave your credit cards at home and only take enough money for what you need for your activity.

• *Seek out nature.* Drive out to the country, or someplace where you can hike or enjoy the outdoors. Spending time in nature can help calm you and clear your head. Gardening can also serve this purpose, as can a trip to your local conservatory, park, or zoo.

• *Take a class or join a team* with the money you would have spent shopping. If you feel an emptiness in your life, pursuing an interest can help fill that void. Even better, use some of the things you've bought to complete one of the projects you've set aside for "when you have time."

• *Volunteer.* Some people shop because they like the sense of accomplishment or admiration from others that finding a great new item affords them. Look into other ways you can feel that same sense of accomplishment. If it's not at work, perhaps you could volunteer somewhere where your skills are appreciated.

• *Turn to Appendix B* for dozens of other activities that might appeal to you.

CHAPTER 7

CLEARING
THE CLUTTER

RANDY O. FROST, PHD, the Smith College psychologist and researcher I've referenced throughout this book, has said that compulsive hoarding is not a house problem, but a person problem. By that, he means that you can go into the home of a compulsive hoarder and clear it out in a day or two, but unless the hoarder addresses his problems, it's likely that the home will revert back to its original state—if not worse—within a short period of time.

One woman called me for a consultation when, in an attempt to do him a favor, she had her young adult son's apartment cleaned and organized while he was on vacation. She told me that in the past she'd thrown away some of his belongings that seemed like junk to her, and he became angry. Within a few months, of course, his apartment was full of more stuff. The lesson here is that the root of the issue lies not in the state of the home but in its inhabitant's state of mind: None of us can judge what is or is not important to another person.

The need to address why any of us have issues with clutter in our homes (as opposed to only clearing out the clutter) is just as important. Once you've resolved to get a handle on your things, you're likely to run out to The Container Store, buy stacks of new bins and drawers and special space-saving hangers, and get to work sorting through and neatening the clutter. When simple disorganization is the problem, this strategy can work. But unless you do a bit of mental sorting—figuring out what your problem areas are and why they've remained so—and come up with a plan of organization that works with the way you think, you may well be back where you started in a matter of weeks or months (except that now you have a bunch of bins and drawers and hangers adding to the clutter).

That's another reason why it's important for someone struggling with hoarding to participate in their own house clearing. The person who hoards needs to learn how to make better choices about what he will keep and what he will toss (indeed, he needs to *choose,* rather than just default to saving or encouraging others to make the choice for him). He also needs to learn how to organize in a way that makes sense to him—and not simply go by what a professional organizer might suggest—so that he gains confidence in his abilities and reduces the risk of falling back into old habits once the cleanup is done. As rewarding as it is to stand in the middle of a clear, clean, nice-smelling living room after a cleanup, that's not enough to sustain the person who has a clutter problem for very long. Old habits die hard, and new ones slip away easily, especially if he hasn't done the work of addressing the cognitive distortions around his possessions, and learned how to think differently about his things and surroundings.

If you're trying to help a friend or relative who clutters, simply cleaning their space for them isn't the best way to assist. Not only is every person's attachment to her things highly personal, but the new system of organization in a clutterer's home needs to be intuitive. The process of carefully sorting through each item in a pile of clutter can be tedious, of course, but you'll be of the most help if you go slowly and let the clutterer be the one who calls the shots. Your role is to help out with the manual labor of cleaning, and to provide support and encouragement.

If you're a clutterer yourself, my hope is that this chapter will help you begin to make mindful, sustainable changes that will improve

THE FIVE LEAST HELPFUL THINGS YOU CAN DO FOR SOMEONE WHO CLUTTERS

1. Throw out things without the person's permission. Doing so will lead to conflict and distrust. The decision about what to get rid of must ultimately lie with the person who lives in the home.

2. Badger him about getting organized. People do not respond to nagging or adversarial arguments. Offer positive encouragement for things he does get rid of. If a clutter problem is persistent, it's likely that the person may be highly self-critical already. Adding your voice to the ones in his head will only make him feel more overwhelmed. Instead, praise any successes, no matter how small.

3. Communicate your frustration nonverbally. Helping someone declutter can be challenging, but folding your arms, sighing, and eye rolling are all ways of conveying criticism. If you find yourself unable to stop letting your frustrations show, take a break.

4. Tell the person you're helping what items should or shouldn't be important. That will only prompt him to defend the items and feel that you are not looking out for his best interests. It will also result in distracting conversations that will not help to accomplish the task at hand.

5. Organize for the person without permission. You may mean well, but doing it for the person does not allow him to learn how to do it on his own. If new organizational behaviors are learned and practiced, it increases his potential to maintain his success.

your life. This is what I do with my clients: I ask them to really think through why they're holding on to their stuff and what feelings they're afraid might surface if they no longer have those things. The only way to overcome a bad habit is to address the issues underlying the behavior. Simple resolve isn't effective and does not produce long-term results.

THE FIVE MOST HELPFUL THINGS YOU CAN DO FOR SOMEONE WHO CLUTTERS

1. Schedule specific times to help. It will help provide structure to have someone to be accountable to for showing up to declutter.

2. Ask how you can help and let the person direct you. It's fine to offer suggestions, but let her be in charge of the process.

3. Divide up chores and work together, and then set up a reward for afterward (such as a breakfast or coffee date).

4. Show empathy when the person is experiencing anxiety. "I know this makes you uncomfortable. I can see why. However, I think that you can handle it and would like to propose that we try to continue to move forward."

5. Be patient. The clutter didn't happen overnight and isn't going to un-happen overnight.

And neither is the perfect multidrawer organizer (especially if you simply pile stuff on top of it) or a rental storage space that allows you to stash your stuff out of sight. Sometimes clutter is the result of failing to use the systems you have in place, and other times it's the result of having a system that doesn't feel intuitive to you. Still other times, you might have the perfect system, but far, far too much stuff to make effective use of it. In the pages that follow, you'll learn how to get organized as you purge.

HABITUATION MEETS PROCRASTINATION

One of the most frequent questions people ask me about my clients is, "How can someone live that way and not realize how bad it is?"

The answer is habituation. A home doesn't become hoarded over-night; the process is gradual, and thousands of small decisions and indecisions about what to keep ultimately lead to a home so filled with stuff that it can become hazardous to one's health. To the person living there, the change isn't dramatic and the environment feels normal. While a person visiting may be overwhelmed by the strong smell of animal urine, the person living there has become habituated to it and barely notices it, if at all. People simply become accustomed to their living conditions.

Habituation can then lead to inertia, and people who compulsively hoard can become somewhat casual about what may well be an emergency situation. "It's not that bad," "It's a little messy," or "I've been meaning to get to it" are phrases I'm used to hearing, as if we were talking about a few dishes in the sink, rather than bags overflowing with cat feces. Not all people who hoard are in denial about how bad things are, but even those who grasp the gravity of their situation and are alarmed by it feel helpless to do anything about it; if the problem becomes too big, overcoming the feelings of being paralyzed and changing the way they're living feels less and less possible. I realize it may seem shocking that someone could get used to living in such extreme conditions, but all of us become habituated to the familiar things in our lives. One person's perfume is another person's headache; one person's dimly lit room is unbearably bright to another. We all become accustomed to the things that surround us on a daily basis.

Think about that bag of old clothes that's been sitting by the door-way in your home, waiting to go to Goodwill for months. Odds are, it's become part of your surroundings, and you don't even see it anymore. The same is true for the Mardi Gras beads hanging on your doorknob because you had nowhere else to put them, or the recycling that you've been meaning to drive over to the drop-off center. It's easy to become gradually habituated to even more extreme clutter once inertia sets in.

Add to that the very common problem of procrastination, which is impossible to discuss without also addressing perfectionism. People are surprised when I share that many people who struggle with compulsive hoarding have perfectionistic tendencies, and that's in part why their homes have become so cluttered. It sounds incongruous because their homes are about as far from perfect as you can imagine.

The struggle begins when an individual brings an item home. A perfectionist wants to choose just the "right" place for it, but isn't sure where that right place is. Of course, if the home is cluttered, it's even harder to see that precise place. The person will set the item down someplace "just for now" until that perfect spot is located, which never happens. With such a high bar, failure is almost inevitable, and can lead to procrastination. She can't figure out where that perfect spot is, and it takes too much time to think about it, so she keeps putting it off.

Meanwhile, she is bringing more items into the house, and the pattern of disorganization continues as things get dropped in random places, adding to the clutter and perpetuating the problem. The job begins to seem even more overwhelming because now nothing short of rethinking the entire house will make it "right." She may start to think, "Why bother trying to have an organized house if I'm going to fail anyway?" And so the piles and hoard continue to grow.

Procrastination is not just a problem of time management. It is a way of coping (maladaptively perhaps, but coping nonetheless) with fear and anxiety. The person doesn't get to the projects she needs to finish, or does several less-important tasks to avoid having to do the one she is unable to begin, because she is anxious about doing it right or being unable to complete it. The act of putting things off again and again only exacerbates and confirms her feelings of failure and low self-worth, and is, of course, self-defeating.

Procrastination is possible to overcome, but when combined with the attention problems many hoarders struggle with, it can be extremely difficult for them to stay on task. When feelings of depression surface as well, paralysis can set in, making a bad situation worse.

Of course, for non-hoarders, procrastination can still be a significant obstacle to keeping a neat and organized home. And any of us can relate to the fact that there are many more pleasant ways to spend your weekend than cleaning out the garage. If you're prone to putting things off, it's never hard to find something more fun to do than organizing or cleaning. It's no wonder there are so many of us on the clutter continuum.

ANTICIPATE ANXIETY

When I work with people who hoard, I prepare them in advance for some of the feelings that might arise as they go through their things and decide what to keep and what to discard. Joan, for instance, had been raped in her home by an intruder 9 years before she came to see me for help with her hoarding problem. She dealt with the aftermath of the assault as best she could, and turned to her extensive church network for support, but had never received professional therapy. As we went through her home together, we were able to identify how her hoarding behaviors were connected to the attack. The worst area of the house— her upstairs guest room—was so full of clothing and boxes that the door couldn't be opened. It had been her bedroom at that time and had been where the rape had taken place. She had sealed off that room as she had the part of her mind that contained memories of the attack, because it was simply too painful to contemplate. Joan had experienced more than an average number of traumatic events in her life, and while this vicious crime was not the sole cause of the hoarding behavior, the emotional issues surrounding it exacerbated her hoarding significantly.

Once she was ready to begin working on the guest room, we worked slowly and processed many of the painful memories that surfaced. As she went through the clothing that had been hidden away in the room that frightened her the most, she began experiencing the emotions she had been avoiding. With the support of an adjunct therapist who specialized in rape and trauma, she actively processed them. By addressing both her hoarding behaviors and her painful memories, Joan was able to reclaim not only her house, but her life as a whole.

Making decisions about what to do with possessions commonly unearths unpleasant emotions and feelings of anxiety for many people—not just hoarders. It's unrealistic to think that you'll be able to clean and purge without experiencing any kind of difficult feelings, and if you're not prepared for them, it can be even more tempting to give up or become distracted when those feelings arise. What you've been avoiding can be as minor as the anticipated sadness when going through a box of jewelry that belonged to your grandmother. Or it can be less predictable, like the feeling of failure and anxiety you experience when sorting through your financial papers. Just looking at them might make you feel as though you'll never be able to make the right monetary decisions or take care of yourself (which is likely a cognitive distortion).

Moving forward, it's a good idea to prepare for the process of decluttering by acknowledging your vulnerability to accumulating and your difficulty with letting go. Being vulnerable to things doesn't make you a weak person. Everyone has a vulnerability to something. In fact, identifying where your difficulties are and recognizing how they interfere with your life is a sign of strength and courage: It's the first step toward changing the way you live.

Secondly, anticipate that anxiety and unpleasant feelings and memories will surface as you declutter. Knowing that you're likely to experience some struggles—some of which may surprise you—will make it easier to continue toward your goal, whether that is to clear your desk or declutter your whole home. Nobody likes to make tough decisions, and it's tempting to put aside for tomorrow what we don't feel like dealing with today. That's how your home typically becomes cluttered in the first place: You don't want to think about which coat you can live without, so you hang the new one alongside the old ones, to avoid deciding. Do I keep this receipt? The decision to toss a scrap of paper "shouldn't" be a hard one, but it can be if you have to think it through: What if I need it? And if I don't have it, what will I do? It is usually better to address what to do with your possessions in the moment, rather than postponing each decision and allowing your things to pile up so that you have an entire afternoon's work ahead of you when it comes time to clean. But of course that's not always how it works. The feelings that arise for you will depend largely on how sentimental you are about your things, what symbolism you attach to your belongings, and what cognitive distortions prevent you from getting rid of things in the moment.

MINDFULLY EVER AFTER

An important practice during the purging and decluttering process is to remain mindful. By this I mean that it's a good idea to try to be mentally and emotionally present. That entails focusing on the task at hand and allowing whatever feelings may arise in the moment to surface, and relinquishing all thoughts of what's happening in the office, what you're making for dinner later, or which other parts of the house you need to get to tomorrow. Not only will remaining mindful make you more productive, it will help you learn to make good decisions about your things on the front end next time, before clutter can accumulate.

The concept of mindfulness includes being nonjudgmental toward yourself and observing your thoughts as they arise without deeming them good or bad. If you've been procrastinating about decluttering your space, there's likely something you've been avoiding about the process—avoiding taking the time, perhaps, or avoiding the feelings that may come up as you begin to sort through your things. Approaching the process with an attitude of self-acceptance ("Whatever comes up for me is okay—I don't need to control the thoughts") will make the process more effective because you are not spending time feeling bad about your feelings. For example, if you go through your refrigerator and purge expired food, you might experience thoughts of being careless or wasteful. If you are mindful as you clean, you can notice these feelings without letting them bring you down. Being present in the task and not judging what has happened in the past allows you to move forward with the positive steps you are making.

Being mindful when decluttering will also help you recognize and disprove your own cognitive distortions, the ones that are keeping you in a cluttered state, both emotionally and physically. Let's say you're cleaning out the refrigerator and come across a head of lettuce that is moldy and watery in the crisper drawer. On top of feeling wasteful, which makes you feel like a bad person (labeling), you might also feel like you'll "never" have a clean refrigerator (all-or-none thinking) because cleaning it will be such an ordeal. In the moment, to avoid dealing with these feelings, it would be tempting to throw the head of lettuce back into the drawer and kick it closed, out of sight and out of mind. But taking a mindful approach will allow you to observe these feelings without labeling yourself or getting caught up in defeatist thinking. The important thing is that the lettuce goes into the garbage, which is a positive step to be acknowledged.

The truth is our stuff can keep us stuck in the past, which robs us of our present. Avoiding things because you want to avoid the emotions that come up prevents you from moving on and achieving your goals of living a healthy, balanced life, both emotionally and physically. The longer you stay stuck, the more you miss out and the more regret builds, and all of these negative feelings ultimately lead to increased avoidance. No one wants to face discomfort. But like many things in life, such as applying for a new job, running a marathon, or losing weight, you will need to do some hard work in order to reap the rewards and take pride in your accomplishment.

WHEN ENOUGH IS FINALLY ENOUGH

If it's hard enough for clutterers to address their disorganized environment, what does that mean for hoarders who need to make a change? Sometimes outside factors like concern from family members, financial debt, or safety issues prompt a hoarder into action. But other times, people who hoard are able to find ways to take action on their own. Habituation and inertia are powerful forces, but I believe that simple human frustration can be a more powerful one. At a certain point, the emotional and physical energy it takes to function in a cluttered environment becomes more frustrating than cleaning up would be, and you simply take action.

This feeling of bottoming out can lead to positive change. It can be extremely powerful. Once you have changed the way you live, you may look back and wonder, "Why did it have to get so bad before I took action?" That's a good question to ask, as long as you keep a positive attitude: I don't believe in regret, but in learning. You might want to ask yourself, "What will I do differently next time?" and/or, "What do I need to do to prevent myself from making this mistake again?" By thinking this way, you allow yourself to move forward in your new way of living.

GETTING STARTED: PLUCK AND PURGE!

What do you do when you've decided that you're sick and tired of being sick and tired, but the clutter is just too overwhelming and makes you want to do anything but dive in? You don't know which room to start in, let alone which area of which room. Here's my step-by-step guide to getting started. Remember: You don't need to do it all in one day. Your goal is to make a difference, not make your home look like a photo from a decorating magazine.

You'll need heavy-duty black (not clear) garbage bags, and three boxes—a "keep" box, a "recycle" box, and a "donate" box. Caution: Some people think it's helpful to have a "decide later" box, but I strongly discourage that. The reason your house has become cluttered is because you've opted to decide later too many times. Now's the time to decide, and with few exceptions, if you can't decide, then consider that you don't need it. (We will get into more detail later about how to make these decisions.) I also discourage listening to music or having the TV on while you declutter, because it distracts you and prevents you from remaining mindful while working.

1. Start with the easiest room to clean first. Decluttering can be overwhelming and it's easy to get discouraged, so you are going to want to have a success right out of the gate that reinforces your decision to take action.

2. Determine how long you are going to work on the room. You can either give yourself a time period, such as a half hour, or you can set a goal, such as "sort through three piles of clothes on the right side of the room." The key here is that you make a commitment to spending a scheduled amount of time on one area or project, and not work beyond your tolerance level. This will be the plan going forward, and you will want to literally schedule times into your week in which you will work in your home.

3. Pluck and purge. When you get started, scan the room to see if there are things that you can randomly start plucking and purging— things that are easy to make decisions about, like garbage, wrappers, or broken items—which will help get the process started, and make room for the things you want to keep. If you come across any junk mail, it goes right into the recycle box. If you haven't gone through it by now, odds are it is expired anyway. There is no need to double-check.

THE OHIO RULE

The OHIO Rule developed by Randy O. Frost, PhD, at Smith College, and his colleagues means: Only Handle Items Once. If you pick up an object, it must go where it belongs, into one of your boxes or into the trash. Don't put it down to decide later. The decision will not get easier by delaying it.

☐ If it's broken, it goes.

☐ If it smells, it goes.

☐ If it's contaminated with bugs, mold, or animal droppings, it goes.

☐ Ask yourself if you have a use for it at a specific point in the future. If not, it goes.

☐ Are you giving it to someone on a set date in the future? If not, it goes.

☐ Does it have a home? If not, then it either goes, or something else does to give it a home.

4. Break up the room. Once you've plucked and purged, you should have a better idea of what is left to do. Let's say you're in the bedroom and you need to clean off the top of the dresser; organize the drawers and get rid of clothes that don't fit; clean off the vanity; go through the night table drawers; organize the bookshelf and DVDs; clean out the closets; get rid of shoes that don't fit; shift your summer clothes to storage and bring out your winter clothes; and figure out what to do with that pile of who-knows-what in the corner. It may just be one room, but that's a lot to do, and it can be very overwhelming to consider all of it at once. Remember, you can either work for a set amount of time (set a timer and do what you can in that time) or pick one area and make that the day's project. There's no right answer—do whatever works for you and feels manageable. Give yourself permission not to get everything done in 1 day.

5. Stay on task. As you go through your chosen section of the room (let's say it's the night table), remember that the night table is the only thing that matters in the moment. Once you pick up an item, you must do something with it (other than put it back down to decide later). If you are keeping it, put it away where it belongs, or if that space is not yet cleared, place it in the "keep" box. Are you donating it? Into the "donate" box it goes. Is it recyclable? There's a box for that. If it doesn't belong in one of these boxes, it's likely that it needs to be thrown away.

One thing to avoid: Try not to leave the room you're working in. If you come across an item that belongs in another room while you're working on your chosen area, place it by the door of the room you're in, and when your allotted cleaning time is up, then you can put away the pile that's accumulated by the door. Otherwise, it's too easy to get distracted and stray off task (you take a glass to the kitchen and realize you're hungry; return a pair of socks to your child's bedroom and are tempted to tidy up her room first).

Be careful, also, not to engage in churning, simply moving something to another room to avoid making a decision about it. That does nothing to reduce clutter. The item needs to be kept and put away (which means there needs to be a place for it), donated, recycled, or thrown away. If there's no place for it, there's a decent chance you don't need it.

6. When you are done with a task and you have more time, either move on to the next one, or save it for the next scheduled purging time. You will get to everything eventually. It's better to pace yourself than to burn out.

7. Act on the three boxes. Put the boxes with the items to be recycled and the items to be donated (seal the boxes so you won't second-guess yourself) where they belong or in your car for a trip to the recycling or donation center. Put the trash where it belongs (no second-guessing yourself here, either—once something is trash,

THE THREE BIGGEST DECLUTTERING TRAPS WE ALL FALL INTO

Below are some common rationalizations that can surface when you begin to declutter your environment. Like all cognitive distortions, they can keep you trapped in a pattern that's not serving you.

The Trap: "I'm afraid I'll need it and regret throwing it away."

The Fear: The regret will be enormous and crippling and will dominate my thoughts. If I have to spend money on another of the same item, I will feel wasteful.

Alternative View: If you haven't used it in a very long time and don't see a specific date by which you will use it, it's very likely that you will never need it. If you do, you can acquire another, either by borrowing or buying it secondhand, if price is a real concern.

The Trap: "I'm afraid I'll never get it back if I throw it away."

The Fear: The thought of making a decision that will permanently affect me is very frightening and makes me anxious.

Alternative View: While you may never get that specific item back, the likelihood of a negative outcome resulting from not having that item is minute. What's more, if you do need it, there may well be a better version of the item available at that time, and in the meantime it won't be taking up space.

The Trap: "My grandmother would have wanted me to keep it."

The Fear: If I get rid of something that someone I loved gave to me, it's like I'm dishonoring her memory and throwing away our relationship and her feelings for me.

Alternative View: You loved your grandmother, and keeping or discarding an item doesn't change that fact. There are other ways of honoring your grandmother than keeping something that takes up space in your home and makes you more overwhelmed. Think of another way to honor her memory and let go of the object.

it's trash). If the items in the "keep" box for that particular room still do not have the space cleared in which you are intending to place them, it's fine to leave them there until that area is available.

8. Acknowledge the progress you've made and give yourself credit. Do not look at all you have left to do. Of course there is a lot to do, but you will get to it. It doesn't have to be perfect, and now is the time to reward yourself for doing something difficult, not to feel discouraged for not having done everything. It takes time to de-clutter a space and learn new habits. If you've done one area, you're doing great. You've taken the first step!

9. Reward yourself. Perhaps you give yourself some time to read a book, watch a movie, or meet a friend for coffee. You've done some-thing that you've been avoiding for months, perhaps even years, so you want to finish feeling good about the experience. Check page 207 for my "Dr. Robin's Love Your Life List," which offers lots of ideas for pleasurable activities that won't add to your clutter.

HONORING THE WAY YOUR BRAIN ORGANIZES

Getting rid of things you don't need and won't use is only part of the clutter-clearing battle. Organizing your space via a method that you will be able to continue is another component (the third is maintaining your new habits, which I cover in Chapter 9). Personal organizer Doro-thy Breininger is very much a believer in working with—not against—the way your mind works.

Everyone thinks about things differently: Some people are more logical and linear in the way they order the world in their minds, while others are more creative; some people rely on visual symbols to remem-ber things, whereas others are more verbal and respond better to the written word.

People who struggle with hoarding often experience difficulty with disorganized thinking and problems with categorization. While most of us would look around our homes and see different categories of clutter—a pile of laundry in need of washing, a stack of mail waiting to be sorted, and perhaps some photographs that could be organized and placed in scrapbooks—someone wrestling with disorganization in their thinking might not be able to sort these items into three separate categories. That person might simply see all these items as "things that need to be dealt with," and they'd wind up with one big pile of stuff.

I worked with a woman years ago who struggled with clutter. We organized her kitchen cabinets together by a method that made sense to her. Rather than putting all the canned goods together on a shelf, she found it more intuitive to group food items by other categories. On one shelf, for instance, she grouped together dessert items— boxes of cake mix, cans of fruit, bags of sugar and flour, and tins of homemade cookies. She also placed ingredients she used to make soup (beans, chicken stock, etc.) together, even though the beans could be used for things other than soup. She frequently made soup, so that's where she'd most likely need the beans. This way of organizing was the strategy that worked best for her.

The point is to have a system that makes sense to you, and that accomplishes your goal of reducing clutter and having predictable places where your things can be found. Someone else might not think it makes sense, but if it works for you, that's all that matters. The idea that there is one "right" way to organize can lead to frustration and paralysis, especially among perfectionists, and is a trap. Dorothy points out that some people need to see their things to know where they are. "There are some people who can put 40 files away and put a Post-It in their calendar on the day they need to go through them that says, 'Tax files in the left-hand drawer, go through them on the 14th,'" she says. But for a person who needs to see his things to remember that they exist, filing things in a closed drawer can be an exercise in frustration.

Not only will he forget where he put things, he will forget that he even has them, and his system will cause ongoing stress and disruption and perhaps even feelings of failure. Her advice is to do whatever comes naturally to you—as long as there is a system and it accomplishes your goal of knowing where things are, it minimizes your emotional clutter. An alternative solution for someone who needs to see things is to use a shelf system. If you're someone whose clothes are scattered all over your room, it may be that you have the wrong system for the way your brain works—you need to see your clothes to know what your choices are, and so you don't like to put things into drawers. The key is to find a system that is visually based, so you are organized while still being able to see your things.

One note about bins, dividers, and other organizational strategies: Ironically, the kinds of organizing tools that seem like they'll be able to solve all of your problems can sometimes feed your clutter problem, rather than mitigate it. I have a client, Serena, whose son is 6 and is showing early signs of hoarding tendencies. My client has a history of anxiety in her family, and while she doesn't struggle with compulsive hoarding, her son, who sees value and beauty in many items that most people would consider trash, has tremendous difficulty throwing things away. If he spots a yellow plastic bead that fell off a necklace into the cracks of the sidewalk, he'll insist on taking it home even if it's dirty or broken. There it will sit on his dresser, along with a piece of Styrofoam that fascinated him, a torn butterfly he cut out in kindergarten, a bird's feather, and a broken plastic top he got from a birthday party goody bag. When Serena encourages her son to resist bringing home these items, she is met with extreme anxiety and tears, so she gives in.

Serena tried to talk her son through each item as they cleaned his room together, but it was a struggle to get him to part with anything and resulted in a tantrum. So Serena went out and purchased several sets of plastic drawers of various sizes to help organize her son's things, so at least they wouldn't be cluttering his room. The problem is that

WHAT KIND OF ORGANIZER ARE YOU?

Everyone has a different method for organizing their things. How do you know which system will work best for you? Here is personal organizer Dorothy Breininger's strategy for determining what kind of organizer you are.

1. Locate your junk drawer. Most people have one—that drawer in the kitchen with the random batteries and foreign coins in it, or maybe it's your bedside table or a drawer in your desk.

2. Pull it out and dump the contents on the floor.

3. Do not think about how you should sort it. Instead, allow yourself to sort it in a way that naturally makes sense to you.

4. Notice how you've sorted things. Did you put the cold medicine, aspirin, and toiletries together; the napkins and plastic forks together; the paper clips and highlighters together? Then you're someone who organizes like with like. Or maybe you put the paper clips, aspirin, and tacks together in one pile of small things and grouped larger items like scissors and staplers in another pile because organizing by size makes the most sense to you. Or you might organize by shape or color or frequency of use. That's fine—as long as it makes sense to you, and you know where to find things.

5. Once you've figured out what kind of an organizer you are, use the information beginning on page 163 to guide the way you declutter your home.

Knowing what kind of organizer you are will enable you to set up a system that works for you. For instance, if you're the kind of organizer who needs to see things to know you have them, then shelves (as opposed to drawers) and clear plastic bins are your friends. Stack files in a horizontal inbox, or use those graduated file stands, rather than a closed file system in a drawer. If you're more color oriented, putting away kids' toys according to color (red trucks, blocks, and balls go together) will make sense to you. You might also want to hang your clothes according to their shades, rather than by category like "dresses" or "tops."

his room already has shelves of bins and dividers and plastic drawers containing all of his other treasures, and the more organized Serena tries to make his room, the more room she is actually creating for him to bring in more things. It's a Catch-22, because if she doesn't organize, her son's clutter will quickly overwhelm them. But if she does, she's

THE BIGGEST ORGANIZING MISTAKES (AND HOW TO AVOID THEM)

Personal organizer Dorothy Breininger says the following issues are traps for many of her clients.

1. Overorganizing. Putting too many layers on things (a finances hanging folder with subcategories for each type of investment account, sub-organized by year, for example) in an ambitious attempt to be perfectly organized can backfire because it's hard to maintain. Keep it simple.

2. Kidding yourself. If you're the type of person who drapes clothing over chairs, it's doubtful that you're going to maintain an elaborate system in your closet with sections for different seasons and fancy space-saving hangers you'll need to wrestle with. Better to put 10 hooks in your closet and hang things on them—your clothes will be off the floor and off the chairs, and it'll be a system you can maintain.

3. Expecting your system to run itself. You can have a great system set up, but if you fail to maintain it, it's not going to help you. Let's say you have folders on your desk with bills clipped, and business receipts. T you'd file the bills that were busin and clip the coupons weekly so wallet. If you simply drop them i through them each week, they what you need when you need it, through the trouble to set up the enabling him to fit in more stuff, and preventing him from confronting and exploring the reasons he feels compelled to do this.

Fortunately, children (and adults) who have hoarding problems or tendencies can often be taught different ways of managing their anxiety before their habits get too entrenched. In Serena's case, talking her son through why he cannot bring certain items into the home ("That bead is dirty and damaged") is critical so he learns what is valuable and useful and what is not. But simply explaining won't always work with kids, who are often too young to be able to understand and apply logic. With young children, you can make cleaning into a game—how fast can we figure out which magic markers still work?—or challenge them to sort objects by how old they are. Making it fun can help increase their motivation to participate and decrease anxiety.

Children who have hoarding tendencies are at risk for becoming compulsive hoarders later in life, but they can learn to address the reasons why they accumulate and participate in their own treatment. The principles are the same: The child must be gently encouraged to think through the thought distortions that are leading to his keeping items he doesn't need and won't use, and learn to resist the behavior. I find that with children, a sticker chart helps: Every time he resists bringing home an item he doesn't need, he gets a sticker. And if he is unable to resist, he must discard something else. Habits become ingrained in children early, but they can also learn to form new habits and prevent problems such as hoarding from continuing into adulthood.

WHEN YOU JUST CAN'T DECIDE ABOUT AN ITEM

When I work with people who struggle with compulsive hoarding, I encourage them to go through their possessions carefully and question their beliefs about why they need to keep specific items. But when you have excessive amounts of clutter to sort through, lingering over decisions about whether or not to keep any one item will only add to your frustration level and the amount of time you spend on decluttering.

Dorothy and I have created a list of questions to help you weigh the relative importance of any item so you can make these decisions quickly and keep moving forward. Ask yourself the questions below, in the given order, and answer yes or no as honestly as you can (try not to overthink your answer). The examples I give are based on decisions that need to be made when sorting through your clothing, but you can use these questions to help you determine whether or not to keep any type of item.

1. *Is it functional?* Let's say you're deciding whether or not to keep a sweater that you like, but which has been attacked by moths and now has several holes in visible areas. Unless you're the kind of person who has a history of taking things to be fixed and then using them, the odds are you're not going to wear that sweater again. Many of us have good intentions to make repairs, but very few of us actually do it. If you're not one of those people who take clothes to the tailor to be rewoven, it's not likely you're going to suddenly become that person. Ask yourself: Is it functional? If the answer is no, it goes. If the answer is yes, proceed to question 2.

2. *Do you love it?* Think about it: You have your sweater, and it's a perfectly nice sweater, but it's not your favorite sweater. When the time comes to get dressed in the morning, how likely is it that you're going to choose to wear the sweater that you don't love? You have one body and many choices for things to cover it. Ask yourself: How likely is it that I'm going to pick something I don't love to perform that function? If the answer is not likely, it goes. If the answer is likely, proceed to question 3.

3. *Is it a classic or utilitarian item?* There is an exception to the *Do you love it?* rule, and that's when an item is a classic (a plain black cardigan, for instance, may not inspire love, but will be worn regularly and would have to be replaced if you get rid of it). The same goes for seldom-used items that you do, in fact, need and are glad to have, like a lobster pot or an exercise mat. Ask yourself: Is it a classic, or will I have to buy another when I need it—and I know I will need it at some point? If the answer is yes, it stays. If the answer is no, proceed to question 4.

4. *Is there a worthy story attached to the item?* Let's say the sweater was the one you were wearing the night you first met your husband, and he spilled wine on you and then proceeded to try to mop it off in the most awkward, charming manner that made you fall in love with him. That's a story that may make a sweater you don't wear worth keeping. But if it's a sweater your sister-in-law got you at Macy's for Christmas 3 years ago and it just doesn't inspire you to want to put it on, it may not be a worthy story. Ask yourself: Does it have a worthy story? If the answer is no, it goes. If the answer is yes, proceed to question 5.

5. *Does the story make you feel good?* If, when you see the sweater, you're reminded of what you adore about your husband, and it makes you smile, that's a great reason to keep it. If you and your husband split up and seeing it makes you feel unhappy, the fact that it has a good story behind it probably doesn't make it worth keeping. Ask yourself: Does the story make me feel good? If not, let it go. If it does, proceed to question 6.

6. *Is the item relevant to your life?* Are there half a dozen other things that you like better than the sweater that remind you of what you love about your husband, such as a photo of him smiling on a recent vacation or the wood carving he made for you that you keep on your desk? If so, perhaps an old sweater that you don't wear can go, because you have something better that serves the same purpose. Ask yourself: Is it still relevant to my life today? If not, it can go. If it is, then you can keep it.

WAYS TO KEEP THINGS WITHOUT KEEPING THEM

In the treatment of compulsive hoarding, I often discourage clients from photographing items as they get rid of them in order to "save" the item without physically saving it. Even though a photo of an item takes up less space than the item itself, I encourage them to get rid of it without a photo as part of their exposure therapy: It's important that they experience the anxiety of letting go of an item, to learn that they can handle letting it go.

In the case of non-hoarders, however, there's nothing wrong with "keeping" an item that's important to you by taking a photo of it, as long as it's not causing clutter. Dorothy recalls working with a woman who had a piano in her living room. It was a large, old piano and no one in her family ever played it, but the woman told Dorothy that she would hate to get rid of it because it had been her mother's, and her mother had always wanted her to learn to play it. She felt that if she got rid of the piano, she would somehow be disappointing her mother, who had passed away. Dorothy suggested that they take a photograph of the family sitting around the piano, place it in a beautiful frame, and hang it in the living room to honor her mother and what was important to her. The woman thought that was an excellent idea and was able to donate the piano to a local conservatory where it could actually be used and enjoyed.

Other ways to "save" items without keeping them include making a quilt out of old clothing; using an item for a different purpose elsewhere in the house (a beautiful serving platter you didn't want to eat off could be hung on your wall); framing a treasured item in a shadow box; or rather than saving every bit of art a child creates, framing one piece, and replacing it each year with a new piece in the same frame.

WHAT NEXT?

In Chapter 8, you'll discover how to apply the principles you've just learned in different spaces. Some people have certain rooms in their homes that are more cluttered than others, or particular areas—clothes or financial paperwork—that they have a hard time organizing. As you read through Chapter 8, you will likely see yourself in several of the scenarios; what's important in this process is to take the best and leave the rest. That is, not every bit of advice, tip, or rule is going to apply to you or work well for you. There is no single right way to declutter or organize that works for everyone, so stay close to what feels right for you, and your environment and your mind will feel clearer in no time.

CHAPTER 8

ROOM BY ROOM

EACH OF US HAS OUR OWN UNIQUE clutter issues, but there are some common struggles we all face when it comes to keeping our homes tidy and organized. Because most people tend to have one or more "problem areas" in their homes, I've structured this chapter by locations in and around the home so that you can easily find the advice most relevant to you. Bear in mind, though, that even if you don't have a problem with clutter in one of the areas of your home listed in the pages that follow, it can still be beneficial to read the recommendations in each section to learn more about organizational systems that could work for you.

THE ENTRYWAY, HALL, OR MUDROOM

This is a commonly cluttered area because it's the first place you walk into—it's where you take off your coat and put down your things after you walk in the door—and it's where stuff tends to accumulate. Everyone has different "drop zones" in the house (sometimes it's the kitchen table), but the entryway often contains a random array of things such as rain boots, pet supplies, mail, keys to unknown locks, clothes, handbags, shopping bags, and various other items that are on their way in or out of the home.

While entryways are often small spaces, they have high potential to increase your emotional clutter, because so many of the things we need on a daily basis get lost there. And because we must pass through that area several times a day in order to go about our daily lives, it's especially important that it's organized. Perfectionism and procrastination often play a part in a cluttered entryway, because we think, "I'll just put it here for now" as a means of putting off finding our items the right home.

Rethinking the way you approach this important area of your home can go a long way toward reducing your daily stress level. Personal organizer Dorothy Breininger recommends reconceptualizing the space from one that you simply walk through and throw your stuff in to treating it as a family "message center," a space where family members can check in with one another and easily get the items they need to go about their day.

Here are ways to organize your entryway and cut down on clutter.

• Install hooks. Consider a hook for your keys so that they're always in the same location each time you enter and leave the house. Hooks for other items you use daily (such as dog leashes, reusable shopping bags, sunglasses, and coats) are also helpful.

• Create a family message center. Dorothy suggests using an inexpensive cardboard vertical file and marking a slot for each family member. Any mail or flyer or classroom permission slip that enters the house, any photograph that you want your husband to look at, and any note you want to pass along to your child goes into that person's slot.

• Keep a small, attractive trash bin near the family message center. It should serve as a constant reminder that trash doesn't need to come any farther into your home. Flyers stuck under your door, receipts that were in your coat pocket, junk mail, and other unneeded items that can cause clutter go straight into the bin.

THE FIVE WAYS TO BEAT CLUTTER

Here are personal organizer Dorothy Breininger's top five ways to limit the stuff pileup.

1. Cap it by number. There's nothing wrong with saving multiples of items you're going to use (such as supermarket bags or rubber bands removed from your daily newspaper). But you don't need an endless supply of these items cluttering up your drawers and cabinets. Set a limit for how many of these items you'll keep on hand at any given time (15 is a good one in this case). Anything over that number should be tossed or recycled.

2. Cap it by height. If you keep books and magazines on your coffee table, for instance, limit your reading material by height, such as 5 inches' worth. Anything more than that needs to be shelved or recycled.

3. Cap it by time. If you haven't read your Monday newspaper by Thursday, you're probably not going to—it should be recycled. Create a limit for how long you'll let periodicals sit around your home. If there's a special issue of a particular publication that you want to save, file it away or keep it on your bookshelf.

4. Cap it by bin size. This is a great trick for storing special but ultimately disposable items, such as your kids' artwork. Place the items in a small bin, perhaps one foot deep. Once it is filled, you must go through it and toss all but one or two favorite items. This gives you a time-limited guideline and allows you to keep what you want to keep without being overwhelmed by clutter.

5. Mark your purge days on your calendar. Make sure you go through each room in the house at least once a week and address any clutter you didn't have a chance to attend to in the moment, and ensure that all of your organizational systems are functioning as they should. You'll be far more likely to keep up with your clutter if you set aside time to address it. Don't try to do the whole house in a day though. You will get overwhelmed and likely not complete the task.

THE KITCHEN

Chaos in the kitchen can be frustrating. It is a functional room—you need space in the cabinets and on the counters to be able to store and prepare food—but it is also traditionally a gathering place for family and guests. A cluttered kitchen doesn't allow you to fully take advantage of and enjoy this social meeting spot. Even if your family doesn't often gather in your kitchen, being able to prepare your food in an area that feels clean and organized makes cooking and eating much more enjoyable. If kitchen clutter involves food (and the inability to throw out food that is old or has expired), it's especially important to address the issue because moldy or spoiled food can pose a hazard to your family's health.

Here are some strategies to help you organize your kitchen and cut down on clutter.

• Make a weekly grocery list after fully surveying the contents of your refrigerator and cupboards. When you shop, try not to deviate from this list. Knowing exactly what items you need to create a week's worth of meals and purchasing only those items will allow you to cut down on kitchen clutter significantly.

• Treat yourself and your family as you would guests in your home. If you wouldn't serve something to them, it's likely you wouldn't to you and/or your family either.

• Rethink your concept of waste. It may feel wasteful to get rid of uneaten food or food-storage containers that you're not using, but if you don't have room to keep them, it's wasteful to let them take up space. Plus, their presence in your kitchen is a constant reminder of the fact that you feel as though you've made a mistake by purchasing them.

• If you have a newer, fresher version of a food item, throw out the older version even if it is "still good" in theory. For instance, if you have a half-used box of pasta that's been sitting in your pantry for 2 years and you just bought a box of your favorite brand of pasta at the supermarket, throw away the old, half-empty box. It's likely that you are not going to use it if you have a newer one. If the item is not expired or opened, you can donate it to a food pantry.

• Treat countertops as work areas, not as storage areas. If something doesn't fit into your pantry, cabinets, or refrigerator, then it shouldn't be purchased. Even if you have a small kitchen with little storage space, you can still avoid clutter by not bringing in more items than you have room for. It may require you to make more frequent trips to the grocery store, but having a clean, organized kitchen is worth the extra work.

• Organize your pantry in a way that makes sense to you—and remember that it doesn't have to be perfect. Your goal here is to be able to see what you have and ensure you have easy access to everything you need. Storing foods like rice, cereal, and pasta in clear containers is often helpful for visually oriented people. The same goes for pots and pans and cooking utensils. It might be helpful to store seldom-used utensils in a separate drawer from the everyday knives and spatulas, so you needn't sort through them to find what you need. Likewise for pots and pans; a hanging rack is a good way for those who are visually oriented to store them, and it saves storage space for things that are used less often.

• Consider quality as well as safety. Food kept in the freezer at the right temperature (0°F) is safe to eat, even if it has freezer burn, but the quality and taste suffer the longer it's in the freezer. In cleaning out the freezer, think realistically about the likelihood that you're going to eat an item that is gray and crystallized, even if it is technically safe to consume. If you've passed by frozen pork chops in favor of ones you bought more recently, it's likely that you're not going to eat the older ones. You deserve to eat food that tastes

(continued on page 170)

HOW LONG CAN FOOD BE SAFELY STORED IN THE REFRIGERATOR?

Clearing clutter in your refrigerator can be a tempting task to put off—you open the door, take a look at what's inside, and simply want to close it again. The chart below will help you make quick decisions about what to keep and what to toss.

STORAGE TIMES FOR REFRIGERATED FOODS

Ground Meat, Ground Poultry, and Stew Meat

Ground beef, turkey, veal, pork, lamb	1–2 days
Stew meats	1–2 days

Fresh Meat (Beef, Veal, Lamb, and Pork)

Steaks, chops, roasts	3–5 days
Variety meats (tongue, kidneys, liver, heart, chitterlings)	1–2 days

Fresh Poultry

Chicken or turkey, whole	1–2 days
Chicken or turkey, parts	1–2 days
Giblets	1–2 days

Bacon and Sausage

Bacon	7 days
Sausage, raw, from meat or poultry	1–2 days
Smoked breakfast links and patties	7 days
Summer sausage labeled "Keep Refrigerated"	Unopened, 3 months; opened, 3 weeks
Hard sausage (such as pepperoni)	2–3 weeks

Ham and Corned Beef

Ham, canned, labeled "Keep Refrigerated"	Unopened, 6–9 months; opened, 3–5 days
Ham, fully cooked, whole	7 days
Ham, fully cooked, half	3–5 days

Ham, fully cooked, slices	3–4 days
Corned beef in pouch with pickling juices	5–7 days

Hot Dogs and Lunchmeats

Hot dogs	Unopened package, 2 weeks; opened package, 1 week
Lunchmeats	Unopened package, 2 weeks; opened package, 3–5 days

Deli and Vacuum-Packed Products

Store-prepared (or homemade) egg, chicken, tuna, ham, and macaroni salads	3–5 days
Prestuffed pork, lamb chops, and chicken breasts	1 day
Store-cooked dinners and entrées	3–4 days
Commercial-brand vacuum-packed dinners with USDA seal	Unopened, 2 weeks

Cooked Meat, Poultry, and Fish Leftovers

Pieces and cooked casseroles	3–4 days
Gravy and broth, patties, and nuggets	3–4 days
Soups and stews	3–4 days

Fresh Fish and Shellfish

Fresh fish and shellfish	1–2 days

Eggs

Fresh, in shell	3–5 weeks
Raw yolks, whites	2–4 days
Hard-cooked	1 week
Liquid pasteurized eggs, egg substitutes	Unopened, 10 days; opened, 3 days
Cooked egg dishes	3–4 days

Source: The United States Department of Agriculture Refrigeration & Food Safety Fact Sheet

good, even if you made the mistake of buying too much of it so that some of it has spoiled or been damaged by freezer burn. Part of getting a handle on clutter is thinking about the kind of life you want to be living, and in all likelihood that's one in which your food is enjoyable as well as safe.

THE LIVING ROOM OR FAMILY ROOM

Few of our living or family rooms look like the perfectly serene pictures we see in furniture catalogs, and for good reason: Those rooms aren't real, and no one lives in them. It's a nice idea to have a vase of flowers and a book of photography artfully arranged on your coffee table, but most of our coffee tables are covered in magazines, remote controls, coasters, and various other odds and ends. The living room is where families congregate, and keeping it uncluttered can be an ongoing challenge. If your living room doubles as a family room, at any given time you're likely to find toys, games, reading material, and backpacks with school supplies spilling out of them thrown down on the couch.

In some homes, the living room is a formal room and is decorated more carefully than other parts of the house. This is where many people entertain, and if your living room is used less often than other rooms in the house, everyday clutter is not so much the issue as the room becoming a museum of sorts, housing artifacts and knickknacks you don't know what else to do with. Too many of these, of course, create clutter. Oftentimes the living room contains our grandmother's Depression glass vase, or our great aunt's antique clock—in other words, things you would probably not have chosen for yourself. These family heirlooms may have been passed down through the generations, but they can also create a lot of clutter on tabletops, mantles, and other areas. Remember, just because an item is old or came from a family member doesn't mean it's truly valuable and meaningful to you.

No matter how you use your living or family room, what's important is that people feel comfortable in the space and that the stuff in the room is there to further the purpose of the room. Anything that isn't pleasing to look at or functional should be relocated. Tips for clearing your living or family room of clutter:

• Ask yourself: Do the items in your living room please you to look at, or have you displayed things in a way that you think will please your visitors? Does that ceramic figurine on the mantle make you happy, or do you feel like it's not your taste but you'd feel guilty getting rid of it? Our living rooms should be attractive spaces for entertaining, but the most important thing is that the room is attractive and functional for you.

• Reconsider what "value" means to you. You might have an expensive painting that doesn't particularly go with the decor in your home. It is worth a lot of money, or would be if you sold it. But you don't care for it, and you are not planning on selling it. So what value does it have, in reality? Unused and unsold, probably not much. It may even make you feel uncomfortable, like you "should" like it, because it was expensive. I would encourage you to think about the item's value to you personally—do *you* like it and does it add to the environment you want in your living room? If not, consider selling it or pass it along to a family member or friend who might enjoy it.

• Take care of what you are getting rid of right away, putting it into the trunk of the car or calling the friend you're giving it to and asking her to come pick it up as soon as possible. If it sits, it will likely be reabsorbed by the room and become part of the clutter again. What's more, the longer it remains, the more likely you are to second-guess your decisions to give it away or donate it.

If this is the room where your family spends the most time together, insist that each member adopts the rule in effect in national parks:

Whatever you come in with, you need to carry out. It's reasonable to designate the family or living room as a place where only shared items—such as the TV, photo albums, and other objects the whole family can use—live. Personal items such as skateboards or books should return to the owner's bedroom when they're not being used. Food, dishes, and other kitchen items must be returned promptly.

THE HOME OFFICE OR WORKSPACE

Papers, papers, and more papers! Some people's offices look as though they house the archives of an entire country. I once worked with a woman named Darcy, who was a doctor. Her home was otherwise not cluttered, but her office was swimming in papers—stacks and stacks of files, binders, and cardboard file boxes filled every inch of the room. Her desk was covered with papers, and while she had files, there was no obvious system in place.

The problem had started a decade earlier when she was writing her dissertation, and much of her research material was in the form of photocopied documents, articles, and papers. She also kept every draft of every article she has ever written, as well as the many versions of her dissertation. "I felt that I might be able to do something with them, somehow use the different drafts in some way eventually," she told me.

Darcy felt uncomfortable and anxious when she considered getting rid of her notes and research. She worried that if she were suddenly called upon to provide proof of her arguments, she wouldn't be able to do so without these papers—even though her dissertation had long ago been published and no one had asked her for backup. She also thought she might be able to use the research for an article she might write in the future and didn't want to risk losing these documents she had once worked so hard to locate.

While her clutter caused her stress because she struggled to find what she needed, Darcy, who was organized and disciplined in most other areas of her home and her life, just couldn't seem to get her home office in order. The task was so daunting that she didn't know where to begin. "There is just too much stuff to organize. The more I have, the more difficult it is to create a system," she said. The problem, of course, was intensified as time passed and more paperwork was generated, increasing both the amount of clutter and Darcy's frustration.

Darcy's office mirrors that of hundreds of people I've worked with. Walking into such a chaotic space day after day can drain your energy and your will to conquer the clutter. Your home workspace should allow you to catch up with your work without having to actually go into the office—it should be a space that feels positive and productive. But when you walk into a cluttered home office, it's likely that you dread having to work from home.

I believe that disorganized home offices are largely a result of the fact that most of us don't know what is reasonable to toss and what needs to be kept. That, combined with the cognitive distortions that arise around the items we keep in these spaces, makes the home office a prime clutter spot.

Darcy's biggest struggles were that she felt overwhelmed at the size and complexity of the task and didn't think she had the time to devote to completing it. She was also anxious about letting go of documents she thought she might need in the future. These feelings are very common for people who have home offices, and quite often lead to paralysis. But if you take the time to clear the clutter from your home office, you'll find yourself far more efficient and the work you do there more pleasurable.

Tips for clearing your home office of clutter:

• *Schedule a work day to organize and purge your home office.* The rest of Darcy's home was in good order because she made decisions about whether to toss or to keep items and where they should go as they came into the house. Her time in her office, however, was designated work time, and she felt she had to focus on "working" while in that room—she didn't have spare time to get organized or put things away properly. If you consider it part of your job to make your workplace the most efficient it can be, it will save you time and effort in the long run, and make you a more efficient worker.

• *Focus on the Greater Good.* Few of us enjoy big projects like tackling the clutter in our home offices. Almost anything seems more important in the moment than decluttering. That's when you need to remember the larger goal, in this case less stress and a calm and organized work environment. Darcy's three Greater Good concepts were: wanting every room in her home to be organized; wanting to feel better about herself; and wanting to have a more pleasant place in which to work. Ask yourself what Greater Good you would benefit from if you got your home office in order.

• *Reframe self-defeating talk as success.* As we were sorting through her papers, Darcy made comments like, "I hate this" and "I can't believe I let it get so bad." I validated her feelings that what she was doing was hard and that it was understandable that she hated doing it. But I also encouraged her to consider that negative comments about the condition of her home office only resulted in her feeling worse about herself. We focused instead on the progress she'd made, and what she was doing to prevent the clutter from accumulating again.

• *Acknowledge that you may, in fact, lose something you need.* Sometimes when you do a major cleanup, you accidentally throw away a document you meant to keep—but it is never the tragedy that you anticipated it to be. You'll work through the situation and figure out a solution to the problem (locate a replacement document, or live without it). Realizing that you can manage your feelings if you lose one piece of paper will actually help you feel less anxious about getting rid of your clutter in the future.

• *Pluck and purge before creating a system.* Instead of going out and buying bins and files and storage drawers and then tackling the room, spend some time plucking and purging. By this, I mean stand in the space and first collect the things that can definitely go. These include trash, junk mail, broken items, and things you've been meaning to give away but haven't. In so doing, you'll make room for what you do want to keep, as well as give yourself space to organize. If there's too much stuff, it's hard to tell what kind of system you even need, so make sure you get rid of enough so that you can evaluate what kind of system makes sense for you. Darcy at first thought there was nothing that could be thrown out, but once she got into the process of plucking and purging, she found that there were many things she didn't really need. That success built her confidence.

• *Keep your system simple.* Many people who compulsively hoard have such optimistic and elaborate ideas of what their organizational system needs to look like that they become paralyzed by inaction. A system doesn't need to be complicated. You could create a simple, color-coded filing system (red folders for interviews, blue folders for drafts of papers, green folders for financial documents, for example), or you can organize your documents alphabetically, chronologically, or by category—however you best remember things.

• *Question your thought distortions.* Darcy held on to each draft of her various papers and said she didn't want to discard things she may later need, but the reality was she also felt a deep emotional connection to these papers, which for her represented years of hard work. To discard them felt like discarding those many hours of work and research, and the recognition she received along with it. We talked about this concept, and when we questioned it, she saw that she was basing her decisions about

(continued on page 178)

ESSENTIAL DOCUMENTS

Not sure what documents you need to keep—and for how long? The following guidelines from personal organizer Dorothy Breininger will put your mind at ease about what documents to hold on to and which you can safely get rid of.

1. Official government documents, such as birth or death certificates, divorce and custody agreements, military discharge papers, adoption records, passports, and social security cards: Always keep, and consider storing in a safe-deposit box.

2. Pension plan information from current and former employers: Keep these indefinitely.

3. School transcripts, diplomas, and report cards: Keep transcripts only if you might seek further education, and keep diplomas indefinitely (although any school you attended should have a record of your graduating). Report cards from childhood are considered memorabilia, and there's no practical reason to keep them.

4. Health records: Keep records of children's immunizations and any hospital records indefinitely.

5. Estate materials: Keep wills and trusts indefinitely. Keep a copy and put the original in a safe-deposit box.

6. Tax returns and receipts: Retain for 6 years. The IRS can audit you up to the past 3 years, 6 if they suspect a large reporting discrepancy.

7. Property records, such as mortgage applications, deeds, loan agreements, etc.: As long as you own the property; save proof of loan payoff indefinitely.

8. Home improvement records and major appliance purchases: Keep all receipts and proof of costs, as well as contracts, as long as you own the property or as long as you still have the appliance, plus 6 years if you wrote off any of the improvements on your taxes.

9. All other receipts from purchases: If you're not sure you're keeping the item, clip the receipt to the item immediately so it doesn't get lost.

If you need the receipt for your taxes, put it in a current year tax folder; if it's for an appliance under warranty, keep it with the warranty. Otherwise, it can go.

10. Warranties, guarantees, and manuals: Keep as long as you own the item. You can toss manuals for appliances that you know how to use.

11. Car or homeowner insurance: Four years after the policy expires or until you get a new one in the mail.

12. Bank statements and credit card records: Only as long as there might be a tax issue (if you need a canceled check to prove a tax write-off, for instance, keep that for 6 years). Keep CDs until they mature. If a bank statement does not contain anything you'll need for your taxes, you can shred it immediately.

13. Bank receipts and deposit slips: Shred after you reconcile your monthly statement.

14. Investment and retirement account statements: Many of these are cumulative, so your year-to-date is reflected on the most recent statement. Unless you want to be able to track the activity of your account, there's no need to keep more than that, especially since you can get records from the investment firm. Keep annual summaries, although even those are available electronically.

15. Pay stubs: Keep in a folder until you get your W2 or 1099 form from the IRS and can reconcile them.

16. Paid bills: As soon as a bill has been paid, consider shredding it. The only exceptions to this rule are if you need the bill as evidence of a charitable contribution or for some other tax purpose (in this case, save it in your tax folder), or if you used a credit card for a purchase that's under warranty.

17. Medical exam results: Consider saving these if there was an abnormality. Remember, your doctor will have the records as well.

keeping her documents on a belief that wasn't accurate. Getting rid of articles she no longer had any use for didn't discredit her hard work. In the end, she decided that she needed to keep only the final versions of the articles.

• *Start scanning.* If you don't have a scanner, consider borrowing one and digitizing your documents. If you don't have time to do it yourself, it's the perfect job for a tech-savvy teenager. You can put everything on disks and back it up on an external hard drive so you'll be doubly covered should you need anything. The way you organize things digitally can also be very simple—by date, by project, whatever works for you. Then you can toss the papers, since you can always print them out again if you need them. There are very few things you need original documents of.

• *Start shredding.* The junk mail that comes along with your bills is a major source of clutter, says Dorothy, and is highly likely to be completely useless, so it should go right in the shredder. As for financial documents that you no longer need, those too should be shredded. Many statements and tax documents contain account numbers and other personal bits of information that are valuable to an identity thief. It's always a good idea to shred these rather than simply recycling them.

• *Work on one area of the office at a time, and stay focused on the task at hand.* While you're organizing the desk, avoid answering e-mails and reading through the letters or journals you find there. Remember, you are there only to organize.

• *Declutter your e-mail inbox.* Your e-mail inbox can be a frustrating source of clutter, even though e-mails do not take up physical space. I work as a national spokesperson for Hotmail in their efforts to help people combat e-mail hoarding and clutter. Their research has found that the average person juggles three e-mail accounts at once with an average of 200 unread e-mails a week.

This same research discovered that there are approximately 45 million self-described e-mail hoarders. The reality is that people are getting overwhelmed by all of the e-mail entering their inboxes. Information can get buried, and it's hard to know what is safe to delete. Start by consolidating your accounts if you have more than one for work and one for home.

• *Begin deleting conversations.* Within each account, sort e-mails by whom they're from, and start deleting. You can often delete entire correspondences with some people with whom your business is over, or even Facebook alerts. That will help you to make progress more quickly. As for e-mails you're not sure you want to delete because you don't want to lose critical information, create "action required" folders ("action required, salary negotiation," "action required, family reunion," etc.). Mark your calendar with the days you will work on these virtual folders. You can do two or three a day until they're done. I recommend devoting 15 minutes a week to deleting e-mails to keep the project from becoming too overwhelming that you just avoid it.

• *Moving forward, sort through your loose papers and e-mails at a scheduled time once a week or once every 2 weeks.* This is where the Greater Good comes back in: It seems much easier to just drop a bill on the desk or leave an e-mail in your inbox, but how much longer would it take to make a decision about where it really belongs? Making the decision to file a paper in the moment helps you achieve your larger goal of reducing physical clutter, which will in turn reduce emotional clutter.

THE BEDROOM

Our bedrooms are highly personal spaces where we relax, recharge, and take care of ourselves. But when our lives are hectic, it's easy to let these spaces fall into disrepair—we step out of our clothes and leave them on the floor, or leave towels hung over the back of a chair or a door. The thought of cleaning out and organizing our closets and dressers on top of all of that can be overwhelming. Usually it's much easier to just leave the door or drawer closed.

But clearing the clutter from the bedroom can afford you peace of mind and help create a sanctuary in which you can unwind at day's end. The emotional clutter that will be cleared away along with the physical clutter can help you feel more refreshed and in control of your life and environment.

Tips for decluttering the bedroom:

• Set up a sorting station. This can be the bed or the floor, but it's an area to be used only for sorting. If you store anything there, you will wind up frustrated and create more clutter.

• Secure four bins or bags: donate, laundry, throw away, put away.

• Start with the floor and begin to sort. Everything should wind up in one of the above bins or bags. Move on to clothing that's thrown over chairs or on surfaces. Then start with the things that are hanging in the closet. You may want to do one section at a time to keep from getting overwhelmed.

• If an article of clothing doesn't fit, it goes into the donate box. There are many shelters and charities that would really appreciate your gift.

• If you haven't worn an item in a long time, only keep it if it has a truly special history, or if it is a classic. Otherwise, consider donating it. If you hesitate about whether to keep something, it's usually a sign that it should go.

• Decide how you want your bedroom to feel, and exile everything that doesn't fit into your vision. The bedroom can become part workspace, part library, and part storage area, with all the stuff you'd expect to see in those places causing it to be cluttered. I've been to many homes that had stacks of read paperbacks on the night table or extra sheets that didn't fit into the linen closet stored under the bed. Try to keep only what you actually use in the bedroom in the bedroom, and you will wind up with a more serene space in which to unwind and may even find it easier to sleep. If you've read a book, pass it along to a friend or move it to the family room bookshelf if you are likely to read it again. Keep the best three sets of sheets you have for your bed, and consider donating the rest or make them into rags. If you need more at a future date, you can get them then. Remember: You don't need to keep something because it has potential to be useful.

THE BATHROOM

Most of us use far fewer toiletries and cosmetic items than we have, but we have a hard time parting with even our unused goods. Those bottles and jars constitute most of the clutter I see in bathrooms. Give yourself permission to throw away an item that you bought with the best of intentions but that is now only cluttering up your bathroom. The guidelines below will help you determine how long it is safe to keep various bathroom items. Be sure to dispose of any products or medications that are past their prime.

• *Medications:* These should be discarded after their expiration dates, and this includes both over-the-counter and prescription medications. Most lose their efficacy and are not dangerous, but especially if you have children in the house, it's a good idea to discard anything that is expired. Mix unused medications with coffee grounds or other garbage to render them unusable to anyone who might be foraging for drugs.

• *Toiletries:* Like most medications, toiletries such as shaving cream or shampoo will not become harmful if they're old, but they may not work to their full potential. Odds are, if you haven't used them in months, and continue to buy a particular brand and use it before you use the bottle that you have in your shower, you're not going to use it. The value of a clutter-free bathroom is greater than having a just-in-case bottle of shampoo that you don't use occupying your bathroom counter.

• *Cosmetics:* Manufacturers are not required by law to put expiration dates on labels, so it's hard to know exactly when to get rid of old makeup. Some ingredients in moisturizers tend to become unstable and lose efficacy over time if they're opened, so if you haven't used an item in 6 months, it's a good idea to get rid of it, simply because even if you do get around to using it, it won't work as well. As for those travel bottles you accumulate from hotels and the like, pack a bag that you can have ready to go for your next trip, and include some there. Whatever doesn't make it into that travel bag gets tossed, or you can bring them (that same day!) to a homeless shelter where they'll be used. Toss any makeup that smells odd, has dried up or separated, or has changed color. Do not keep mascara after 3 months, and never save any eye makeup that you used when you had an eye infection (you can reinfect yourself). Some products do have expiration dates, but if they've been stored improperly or left open, they may contain bacteria even if they aren't expired. Natural products tend to deteriorate faster.

THE CAR

Your car can become the repository of good intentions. At any given time, the trunk or the backseat may contain bags of recycling meant for the recycling center, hand-me-down clothing given to you by your sister for your children that somehow never made it into your house, and tools borrowed and returned to you by a neighbor that need to be stored in the garage. The interior of a car, especially if you have children, may also contain coloring books, magic markers, games and DVDs, and uneaten food or wrappers. Some people's vehicles become mobile storage lockers, containing sporting equipment that is used perhaps 1 week out of the year, but lives full-time in the back of the minivan.

A cluttered car, of course, means a less comfortable driving experience, and on occasion a less safe one. Digging around for a toll pass in a compartment full of papers, eyeglass cases, and cell phone chargers can distract you from the road and become a safety issue. For that reason alone, it's important to declutter your car.

Some tips for a clutter-free car:

• Toss, don't just relocate. When you get in your car, rather than throwing the soda can or other loose items into the back, take the 30 extra seconds to collect and throw out garbage. Also clear out things that don't belong in the car (books you've finished reading, deflated beach balls from last summer, that vase your mother gave you). Bring them inside and distribute them where they belong.

• Set aside a few hours a week as purge time. Go to the recycling center, the food pantry, or wherever it is you've been meaning to bring the things in the back of your car. Trying to fit it in between commutes and drop-offs adds stress to your day, but taking care of things in the moment will make you feel accomplished and help to declutter your car.

• Invest in some inexpensive over-the-seat organizers for the back-seat so children can learn to put away their things rather than tossing them on the floor.

• Place a canvas or nylon bag over the back of one of the seats and line it with a kitchen garbage bag for food or other items to be disposed of. Empty the trash as you would in your home as you leave the car.

• Stay on top of it. Every week go through your car to ensure that there are no items that need to be thrown away or taken inside to be put away.

THE GARAGE AND ATTIC

Attics, garages, and outdoor sheds are where some of the bigger projects go to live indefinitely. They're also where people tend to stash things that they can't bear to make decisions about. Many of the people I work with can't even park their cars in their garages because they're so filled with stuff. Storing items in garages and attics is often an example of churning, or simply moving things from one space to another instead of dealing with them in a more permanent way.

Alexa's stepfather, Robert, whom I wrote about in Chapter 2, is a classic example of someone who churned. He had the space in his home to keep things he didn't need, want, or have a clear plan to use, and so he put these items in boxes or on shelves in his attic, basement, and garage simply because he didn't see a reason to throw them out. If you recall, Robert's house was, in fact, big enough to accommodate all of his things, but when he died, he left behind a lifetime worth of items that he never used.

Another problem with storing things in attics, basements, and garages is that items kept in these spaces tend to suffer from lack of climate control and sometimes even exposure to the elements or to pests. I had a client who stored her daughters' baby clothes in the basement to one day give to her granddaughter, but because the clothes weren't packed and sealed properly, they were irreparably damaged by humidity. Basements are also prone to leaks and flooding, which can create mold problems.

Tips to declutter an attic, garage, or basement:

• Don't simply store stuff without a plan. Many people store items in these spaces that they simply don't know what else to do with. While the attic is the perfect place to keep childhood memorabilia to share with your grandchildren, it's not ideal to store a box of toys that are usable but not especially valuable. It might be better to donate or dispose of them after they've outlived their use.

• Recruit a helper. Ideally this would be someone, perhaps a family member, who would find it fun and interesting to dig through family artifacts. If your helper is a family member, he or she may even be interested in taking some extra items off your hands.

• Find new homes for your stuff. What do you do with the pair of children's snow boots that were worn but not worn out? Or the luggage that works fine, but you have luggage that you prefer to use? Why not sell them on eBay, or post a listing on Freecycle .com, a network made up of people across the country who are looking to pick up free or donated items? If you decide to resell or donate in this way, though, be sure to make time within a week to do so; otherwise, the stuff finds its way back into your house and contributes to the clutter.

• Donate whole collections. Robert, Alexa's stepfather, had an extensive electric train setup in his basement that his son used 30 years earlier when he was a child. Robert kept it for sentimental reasons and even added to it at times, but it lay unused for years. In the end, it went to a children's hospital. It's fine to donate collections of things that once had meaning but no longer do.

• Accept that some things will not be put to use. This includes projects that were started but not completed (model airplane kits, furniture you meant to refinish but just stored). Acknowledging that you were not able to complete a project allows you to move forward to those that you can actually get to.

• Dispose of anything that has an odor or is destroyed by mildew or other contaminants.

OVERCOMING YOUR OBSTACLES

It is the rare person who jumps for joy at the idea of spending the day indoors, dressed in work clothes and making stressful, sometimes

CLUTTER AND PETS

We love our pets, but they do add disorder to already cluttered homes and can create a sense of chaos. I'm certainly not advocating that you get rid of a pet to prevent clutter; my very special bird Luigi, who recently passed, meant the world to me and was worth every bit of work he required. But if you have a pet or are considering getting one, evaluate the impact on your environment before you commit.

☐ Pet hair can be time consuming and difficult to clean up. If you do have a shedding pet, investing in a vacuum that is designed for pet hair can help keep it under control.

☐ Litter boxes require daily maintenance. I recommend linking the act of cleaning it out to something else you do every day without fail, like taking out the garbage. Do it before or after, which will help to reduce the accumulation.

☐ Pet food and accessories add clutter to a home. Just like any other family member, your pet should have a place for his things: a hook for his leashes, a bin for his toys, and airtight containers stored in a designated place for his food.

☐ Properly caring for your pets and maintaining the environment they (and you) live in requires a substantial time commitment. If you already have a difficult time maintaining order in your home, this is an important consideration.

emotional decisions about his possessions. We all come up with excuses to avoid doing what we know we need to do. One of the most common ones I hear is that the person doesn't have the time or would prefer to spend her time with her family. To people who say they don't have time, I answer, "Really? But you have time to go to garage and yard sales, on shopping sprees, and on other tempting acquiring trips? It would be interesting to log how many hours were spent hunting and gathering and compare that to how long it would take to declutter." As I was writing this book, I remember thinking that I didn't have time to write a book. But when it came down to it, I somehow found the time. By asking for help and delegating tasks, I found that the time was there.

And, remember, no one is suggesting that you'll be able to do everything in a single day or do it all perfectly. Many people who struggle with compulsive hoarding and those with clutter issues have unrealistic expectations for themselves. Make a schedule that works for you, and begin to trade some of the behaviors that have led to the problem for behaviors that help to remedy it. If you have a setback—and you probably will—it is not a tragedy. Just dust yourself off and get back on track. As for wanting to spend time with your family rather than decluttering, consider what it would be like to spend time with your family in an ordered, uncluttered environment. As your house becomes organized, you will likely have less stress, less guilt, and more of an opportunity to give your family the kind of quality time that you and they deserve to enjoy.

When people say they don't have the time to declutter, often what they mean is they aren't in the mood or don't want to have to go through the work of making the hard decisions. Maybe they've had a stressful day and don't feel like it, and of course, they have other things they would prefer to do. That's understandable. But if you succumb to those feelings, the clutter accumulates, and that doesn't help your mood or your stress level. While some people are better at persevering when they're not feeling up to a task, almost all of us usually find a way. You can't *not* feed your children dinner because you are stressed, or fail to complete an assignment at work because you're upset with another employee. There would be consequences if you did. It is important to apply this same commitment to getting your house in order. Put those uncomfortable feelings on the shelf and move toward creating change. It's been my observation that when clients give themselves a little distance from those feelings, and can do something positive in the meantime, they will feel better about themselves and the situation, and perhaps determine a different response than they might have had otherwise.

Lack of storage space or the right kind of shelving is another common excuse for not decluttering. Decluttering is not about making more room to accommodate all your stuff by finding space in closets, makeshift storage bins, or those plastic vacuum-packed storage bags that you see on TV. You're looking to make your home comfortable and livable, relaxing, and peaceful, one that is pleasing to the eye and that doesn't contain so much stuff that you can't access what you need. Instead of thinking about where you're going to put everything, think about purging what you don't use or need and seeing what's left over. In the future, focus on controlling what comes in. This will help you to determine whether you truly do or do not need more shelving, or room to place items.

The truth is that defeatism is often at the root of these thinking patterns—"No one will help me"; "I don't know where to start"; or "What's the point? It'll just get messy again." And it's understandable that you might feel overwhelmed before you even begin. Trying to change habits can be a long, exhausting process. There's nothing wrong with acknowledging that you've had difficulty in the past. But now, you have new tools that you didn't have before. I am frequently reminded that most people who have cluttering or hoarding problems don't truly know how to go about clearing the clutter and changing their behavior. It's really no different than sitting down in front of a new computer program or trying to operate a piece of machinery you've never seen before without any instruction. You're not expected to intrinsically know how to solve this problem. This is where you need to give yourself credit for trying, and to put into action the concepts you've been learning in this book.

In fact, rather than thinking about the past, consider moving forward to the future. It's time to start looking at what you can do, not what you can't. You will have struggles, and you'll feel like giving up. But remember, those feelings are temporary and have only as much power as you give them. It may be a cliché, but it's true: Take one step at a time, or in this case, get rid of one item at a time.

CHAPTER 9

KEEPING YOUR LIFE CLUTTER-FREE

BY NOW YOU'VE COME TO understand that overcoming compulsive hoarding is not simply a matter of willpower. The condition is complicated and is the result of many factors, including learned behaviors, trigger events in one's life, cognitive distortions, and issues related to brain chemistry, and treatment requires a multifaceted approach with tremendous support from others. While a strong will and motivation are necessary elements for any type of change, these factors alone are not enough to combat the thoughts and behaviors that drive compulsive hoarding. The same is true, albeit to a lesser degree, for those of us on the lower end of the hoarding spectrum. Just because we fill up several garbage bags' worth of unwanted stuff doesn't mean we've conquered our clutter problem.

The good news is that maintaining the environment you've worked so hard to create will not be as difficult as it was to confront all of the issues that led to the clutter. And the other good news is that while keeping your home clutter-free will require regular care and vigilance, once your new habits take hold, they'll quickly replace the ones you've been working to change. In other words, if you work to replace your old clutter habits with new daily choices that help you maintain the life you want, keeping your home clutter-free will get easier and easier. The reward for your actions—having less stress and a calmer sanctuary of a home—will serve as a constant reminder of why you're staying on top of the problem.

As you maintain your newfound strategies of organization and order in your household, it's important to manage your expectations. Clutter and the reemergence of emotional issues can sometimes creep up on you. For the most part, clutter is the result of your reluctance to make a decision about your possessions, and anxiety about those decisions doesn't go away overnight. New decisions are likely to bring new anxiety, and you may need to learn and relearn how to question the cognitive distortions that led you to acquire and keep things in the first place. Like breaking any bad habit, learning how to think about things differently and substitute other, better habits is a process, and setbacks should be incorporated into that process.

I put the word *failure* in quotes above because viewing things as clear-cut successes or failures is a trap that only feeds procrastination and perfectionism. Sometimes my clients don't even attempt to maintain their new sense of order because they fear that if they try, they will fail. It's a common form of self-defeating behavior that many of us regularly engage in. Of course, when we engage in this kind of future-predicting cognitive distortion, we set ourselves up for failure.

You can either prove yourself right, or you can work toward overcoming your problem. Redefining success in this case to be something attainable, and celebrating your successes, small though they may be, sets you up for more success. Expecting a bit of "failure"—that is to say, building room for setbacks and imperfections into your process— is a way of keeping your expectations of yourself reasonable, and to continue moving forward. It's a balance of being patient and compassionate with yourself, thinking realistically, and taking action.

Remember Joan, the woman you met at the beginning of Chapter 1? Her home is a very different place now. While she says she still has some clutter to work on, she's now able to keep her home orderly. Joan says she still struggles with wanting to avoid dealing with her clutter, and has to talk herself through the cognitive distortions, but is now living significantly closer to the way she wants to live. "At first, I didn't think it was possible. But remembering to take baby steps and to be patient with myself and the process allowed me to continue to move forward at a steady pace," she told me when I followed up with her recently.

Now keep in mind that Joan, like many, wanted to give up at many points in the process. As her coach, I was able to give her some verbal reminders that she could call upon when she needed them. "Your house didn't get this way overnight, and it's not going to be fixed overnight" was one that Joan found particularly useful. Joan found it helpful to post some of the more applicable reminders around her house to bolster her when she felt defeated and tired.

THE GREATER GOOD MOVING FORWARD

What looks and feels easiest in the moment can create a lot more work and stress for you in the not-too-distant future. In the instant that you're experiencing anxiety, whether it's about what will happen if you pass up a good deal at a flea market or not wanting to think about the regret you'll feel if you throw something away and need it later, you'll do whatever you need to do to relieve that anxiety—which is usually to avoid the decision.

If you've been engaging in this behavior for years, you know where that gets you: a cluttered house. There's a certain comfort in that predictability—even if it doesn't feel good, you know how it's going to feel. What's not known is how you and your family will feel once you get your emotional and physical clutter in order, and even though that's your goal, it can be a bit stressful to change your behavior and attitudes.

That's where the Greater Good comes in. When you're feeling anxiety or dread about organizing or clearing clutter, or even when you're anticipating feeling anxiety about not being able to buy the things you want on your next trip to the mall, remember that you're working toward a Greater Good that will improve your life in such a way that it's worth confronting and tolerating the anxiety you feel in the moment.

For example, let's say you've just brought home a carload of groceries, and as you go to put them away, you're faced with a crowded pantry overflowing with cans and boxes of foods that you've accumulated over time. All of a sudden, what was a manageable task (putting away the groceries) starts to feel like an ordeal: Now I have to figure out what to throw away and how to rearrange my shelves in order to make room for the new food I bought. Not only might that feel daunting (and you'd rather join your spouse on the couch and watch TV), but you also don't want to face the uncomfortable feelings and thoughts that you're predicting will come up. *Why didn't I plan better? I should have made a list. I'm wasting money on food we don't need and wasting food because things are going to go bad. I don't cook enough, and that makes me a bad wife.* In the end, you probably just decide to stuff in the new food wherever you can and avoid the issue altogether.

All of these thoughts and decisions take place in a split second, and you may not be consciously aware of them. All you know is that you don't feel like undertaking the task, and you choose to do something else. But the downside is that your pantry will be disorganized later when you need to make dinner, and when you wake up the next morning and walk into the kitchen to make coffee. That feeling of anxiety will continue to haunt you. That's emotional clutter. You'll have a harder time figuring out what to make for dinner that evening or finding your coffee filters in the morning because your pantry is overflowing, and your resulting frustration can set you up to feel bad for the remainder of your day.

Here's a different scenario: If, in the moment that you had the choice between avoiding your anxiety by walking away (which,

YOUR GREATER GOOD

☐ My Greater Good is having a better relationship with my spouse because there will be fewer resentments over our living space.

☐ My Greater Good is having more money for things like vacations or those repairs on my house I've been saving up for because I haven't spent it on smaller, spur-of-the-moment purchases that only add clutter to my home.

Now it's your turn:

☐ My greater good is _____.
☐ My greater good is _____.

remember, doesn't really avoid it, but postpones it) or confronting it, you'd reminded yourself of your Greater Good, you may have made a better choice. Let's say the Greater Good in this case is looking forward to preparing a healthy dinner for the people you love. You might then think, "You know, I'll just take a minute to check which cans I have doubles of, and set aside the older ones. Then I can figure out which ingredients I'll need to cook dinner, and put them in the front of the pantry." You will wind up closer to your Greater Good. For that reason, it's worth taking a few minutes now to think about what your Greater Good looks like. I'll start you off with a few examples, and then you paint a picture of your own Greater Good.

WORK WITHIN A SYSTEM

Think of maintaining your environment as a policy: There are things I simply must do because living in a calm, chaos-free home is important to me. Creating a daily system for yourself saves you from having to agonize over your decisions again and again each day. Your policy might include things like: I will make it a point to sort through the mail before dinnertime; or, If I haven't read the newspaper by the time I'm ready for bed, it goes in the recycling bin. Having these kinds of simple rules in place prevents you from backsliding into the behaviors and bad habits that led you to clutter your home in the first place.

Here are five tips that will help keep your system on track.

1. Schedule time every week to complete at least one project around the house. Don't let anything interfere with that appointment, just as you wouldn't let anything interfere with a work appointment or a doctor's appointment.

STOP CREEPING CLUTTER WHERE IT STARTS

Keeping clutter to a minimum requires action on your part, as well as inaction: deciding not to bring something into the house if it has no home, for instance. Here are some tips on how to keep clutter from creeping up on you.

1. Nip clutter in the bud. One bowl in the sink can so easily become a bowl and a glass and then a sink full of dishes. For some people, seeing a dish in the sink creates a sense that it's normal for dishes to be in the sink, and the bar for clutter is lowered. Others will see that someone has left their dish in the sink and add theirs without thinking twice. Soon loading the dishwasher turns into a major project: Doing the Dishes. If you're prone to clutter and procrastination, it's best to make the effort in the moment so a small project doesn't turn into a daunting one.

2. Remember the OHIO rule: Only Handle It Once. If you pick something up, do not put it back in the same place, unless it truly belongs there. Once in your hands, it should go where it lives, into the recycling, into

2. If you are married or live with other family members or even have roommates, consider including those people in your clutter cleanup. Even if it's not their problem or clutter, you might be surprised how important your family feels when they are asked to help.

3. Be a host: Invite a friend to come over once a week for coffee or offer to host book club meetings at your house. Knowing that others will see your home on a regular basis is good motivation to stay on track.

4. Keep a journal that will allow you to track your progress and accomplishments. It is critical that you acknowledge the positive steps you're taking, as it will reinforce your new system and keep

the trash, or to the person it belongs to. If you find yourself picking things up and not actually decluttering, that's the time to put the OHIO rule into effect.

3. Set a daily maintenance schedule. Consider putting 15 minutes aside in your day to go through a problem area (your desk, the kitchen table) and declutter. Set aside a half an hour on the weekend (or on your days off) for things like filing or other more tedious projects. Think of it like brushing your teeth and showering—it's basic maintenance that will keep your environment healthy.

4. Finish what you start. Shopping for groceries includes putting them away. Doing the laundry includes folding it and putting it away. Washing the dishes includes drying them and putting them where they belong. Leaving any job partly undone leads to procrastination and clutter, which begins to feel very overwhelming very quickly.

5. Regroup. If you find that you're having a hard time staying on top of the clutter, go back to the principles covered in Chapters 5, 6, and 7, such as One In, One Out.

you on track. Focusing on what you haven't accomplished is likely to lead you to start cluttering again.

5. Make your reward automatic. In other words, don't decide that a clean space is reward enough. If you've accomplished your goals for the week and stuck to your system, maybe the family gets to enjoy Friday pizza night in your comfortable den, or you all get together and cook dinner in your clean, organized kitchen. Remind yourself of why it's so enjoyable to have a clutter-free home.

A WORD ON ACQUISITION AND AVOIDANCE

Generally speaking, I'm not in favor of avoiding your triggers as a long-term solution to compulsive acquiring. The underlying tenet of cognitive behavioral therapy (CBT) is that in order to change your response to your anxiety, you need to begin confronting the situations that are difficult for you and find ways to manage your anxiety. That's why it's important to face and work through your triggers so you reduce the urge to acquire, rather than simply never going to the mall. That said, keeping a distance from tempting situations may be necessary initially, until you feel you can resist impulse purchases. Being at the wrong place at the wrong time and bringing clutter into your house can set you up to feel defeated.

It's important to anticipate the old patterns you may fall into and plan to avoid them by creating new habits that support your Greater Good. If you tend to shop during your lunch hour at work, for example, set up lunch dates with coworkers or use that hour to go to the gym or walk outside and get some exercise. If you're tempted by the dollar store you always pass on your way home from driving the kids to school, take a different route, and reward yourself by stopping for coffee on certain days instead.

IF THE CLUTTER IS TAKING OVER AGAIN

While I hope that this book took you a long way toward clearing the emotional and physical clutter from your life, sometimes you need more help than a book can provide. There are some powerful reasons that drive people to hoard or clutter, and if you are unable to make changes on your own or just want a bit more support, it can be helpful to see a therapist. Compulsive hoarding, as you know, can come about or be exacerbated by many factors, such as a person's biology, childhood trauma, past abuse, a major loss, or deprivation. These issues can be hard to process on your own.

How do you know when you could benefit from therapy? Consider seeing a therapist if any of the following statements apply to you.

• You're having trouble dealing with the emotions that are arising as you attempt to organize and clean your home, and the sadness or anxiety you're experiencing is interfering with your everyday life.

• You are living with someone who is not supportive of your efforts to improve your home and may be trying to block your success.

• Your relationships with family members are not healthy, and you're not sure how to get back on track.

• You are in a crisis situation (your home is unsafe, for instance) and need immediate assistance.

I very much hope that you've found the tools and information in this book helpful and that you've been able to gain a deeper understanding of your relationship to your possessions, and of your place on the clutter continuum. While I believe we can all agree that possessions are a useful and potentially enjoyable part of life, too much stuff can have both physical and emotional consequences that affect us negatively. I know that the steps you are taking to manage your clutter will result in a more enjoyable, less emotionally cluttered life.

Finally, remember to be kind to and patient with yourself. Change takes time, so give yourself that gift. With an eye toward your Greater Good, you will have a new direction that will have paid off and been well worth the work.

ACKNOWLEDGMENTS

I wish to show my gratitude and appreciation to the following individuals without whom I could not have written a word . . .

Rebecca Gradinger, my literary agent, who had faith in me and who encouraged me to write this book.

Rob Sharenow, Matt Chan, and Dave Severson who believed in me and gave me the tremendous opportunity to be a part of *Hoarders*—the true inspiration behind this book.

George Butts whose kind and gentle nature was always there to help me navigate through some very complicated situations over the past 2 years.

Alice Ikeda and Pat Barnes for being available 24/7 during our shooting schedules. The laughter and fun we shared helped alleviate some of the frustrations during the most difficult hoarding situations.

Michael Tompkins, Joan Davidson, and Fred Penzel, for their much appreciated feedback, support, and encouragement throughout the entire writing process.

Andy Berg at A&E, whose wisdom, advice, and faith in me was amazing. I appreciate the trust you placed in me to keep you safe in your very first hoarder house!

Gina Nocero, for the many successful media opportunities.

Stephanie Dolgoff, who stayed up late at night, helping me to compose this book, and without whom this book would not be possible.

Dorothy Breininger, who contributed her expertise in helping to formulate strategies for those looking to make their lives more organized.

Matt Paxton and Cory Chalmers. We are a force to be reckoned with and The Trifecta!

Stephanie, my very best friend, who never lets me down.

My mom, who was always there—without fail—to comfort me and encourage me when I was feeling overwhelmed.

And lastly, my loving husband, Mike, who gave me unconditional love, put up with my hectic travel schedules, and long nights writing and editing.

APPENDIX A

COMPULSIVE HOARDING
SAVED ITEMS QUESTIONNAIRE

Note the items that you save, and the level of anxiety that you anticipate you would experience if you had to let them go.

Scale: 0 = No Anxiety; 5 = Moderate; 10 = Potential Meltdown

ITEM	DETAILS	ANXIETY LEVEL
PAPER PRODUCTS		
Newspapers _____		_____
Magazines_____		_____
Books _____		_____
Receipts _____		_____
Schoolwork_____		_____
Mail_____		_____
Lists/Notes _____		_____
Recycling_____		_____
Pictures_____		_____
Office supplies_____		_____
Other paperwork _____		_____

ITEM	DETAILS	ANXIETY LEVEL

DIGITAL

E-mails _____ _____

Files_____ _____

Other_____ _____

COLLECTIBLES

Stuffed animals _____ _____

Dolls _____ _____

Barbies _____ _____

Model cars _____ _____

Childhood items_____ _____

Other_____ _____

AUTOMOTIVE

Tools _____ _____

Car parts _____ _____

Cars_____ _____

Cleaning products _____ _____

ELECTRONIC

Appliances _____ _____

Clocks_____ _____

Radios/Stereos_____ _____

Computers_____ _____

Telephones _____ _____

Fix-it parts _____ _____

Other_____ _____

ITEM	DETAILS	ANXIETY LEVEL
HOUSEHOLD		
Linens _____		_____
Plastic food-storage containers _____		_____
Pots/Pans _____		_____
Food _____		_____
Spices _____		
HEALTH		
Medications _____		_____
Facial products _____		_____
Hair products _____		_____
Other_____		_____
ANIMAL		
Pets_____		_____
Pet products _____		_____
HOLIDAY ITEMS		
Christmas _____		_____
Easter _____		_____
Fourth of July _____		_____
Thanksgiving_____		_____
Other_____		_____

ITEM	DETAILS	ANXIETY LEVEL
PERSONAL		
Clothing	_____	_____
Shoes	_____	_____
Purses	_____	_____
Scarves	_____	_____
Other	_____	_____
CRAFT SUPPLIES		
Beading	_____	_____
Scrapbooking	_____	_____
Bins	_____	_____
Stencils	_____	_____
Markers	_____	_____
OTHER:	_____	_____
OTHER:	_____	_____
OTHER:	_____	_____
OTHER:	_____	_____
OTHER:	_____	_____

Now take a few moments to review your answers here, and notice any patterns. Do you have particular issues with written material, for instance? Are most of the items you have a hard time getting rid of things you acquired when they were on sale, or at a particular store? Are the items things that you plan to use for a project that you plan to get to at some future date? Knowing your triggers can give you important insight into why you're saving what you save, and which distortions in thinking might be leading you to do so. See if you can make some connections here, and refer back to Chapters 6, 7, and 8 to find alternative ways of thinking about your things. All of that will make mindfully letting go of your clutter easier, and enable you to maintain a clean, uncluttered space into the future.

Appendix B

Dr. Robin's
Love Your Life List

Staring at a heap of clutter, a pile of laundry that never seems to get folded and put away, or a room whose door you leave closed because you just can't bear to be reminded of the mess you haven't cleaned up can be incredibly discouraging and overwhelming. It's easy to get bogged down in strategizing what to do with your stuff and untangling those thought distortions that keep you from living the kind of life you want.

While doing those things is necessary to clear your clutter, my Love Your Life List is designed to give you something exciting to look forward to as a reward for tackling the problem of the clutter in your life or as a means of substituting one habit that may lead you down the wrong path (such as walking at the mall) with another (like cycling with a friend) that will support your long-term goals.

I've included blank spaces at the end of this list so that you can add in your own favorite activities. Be very specific and make sure your pleasurable activities are things you can do without a lot of planning or work, so they'll be accessible to you when you need them. These are my top 51.

1. Go for a drive in the country
2. Listen to music
3. Spend time with family

4. Go for a walk outside

5. Paint, draw, or do other artwork

6. Play golf

7. Learn a new skill by reading a how-to book

8. Read a great novel

9. Sit down and write your own great novel

10. Write in your journal

11. Watch a movie

12. Go online and connect with friends

13. Go to your local bookstore for a free reading

14. Watch TV

15. Read the newspaper

16. Play cards

17. Complete a crossword puzzle

18. Have coffee with a friend

19. Go to the gym

20. Go for a run outside

21. Bake cookies

22. Open a great bottle of wine

23. Learn to knit or crochet

24. Play with your pet

25. Teach yourself how to make a new recipe

26. Go for a hike

27. Join your church choir

28. Go to the library

29. Make someone a homemade birthday card

30. Attend church

31. Play a musical instrument

32. Stop by a local school and offer to help out in the office or classroom

33. Play chess or checkers with your spouse

34. Donate time at a local soup kitchen

35. Go bowling

36. Plant a vegetable garden

37. Go dancing

38. Buy yourself flowers

39. Visit an elderly neighbor and offer to cut their lawn

40. Get a car wash

41. Meditate

42. Get a massage or back rub

43. Write a letter to an old friend

44. Go on a picnic or have a barbecue

45. Play basketball

46. Take your camera outside and shoot the world around you

47. Get a haircut

48. Go to a museum

49. Go fishing

50. Do yoga

51. Call a good friend

_____

_____

_____

_____

_____

INDEX

Underscored page references indicate boxed text.